PRACTICAL
ALLOTMENTS
PAUL WAGLAND

PRACTICAL ALLOTMENTS

PAUL WAGLAND

GUILD OF MASTER
CRAFTSMAN PUBLICATIONS

Dedicated to Jeannine McAndrew.

First published 2009 by

Guild of Master Craftsman Publications Ltd.
Castle Place, 166 High Street, Lewes, East Sussex BN7 1XU

Text © Paul Wagland
Copyright in the Work © GMC Publications 2009

ISBN 978-1-86108-640-2

Associate Publisher: Jonathan Bailey
Production Manager: Jim Bulley
Managing Editor: Gerrie Purcell
Senior Project Editor: Dominique Page
Editor: Simon Smith
Managing Art Editor: Gilda Pacitti
Design: Chloë Alexander

Set in Nofret and Helvetica Neue
Colour origination by GMC Publications
Printed and bound by Sino Publishing in China

All photography by Paul Wagland, with the following exceptions:

Dreamstime.com: Inavanhateren: 11BL, 24TR, ; Piksells: 24BL; Jmori48: 25B; Gynane: 25TR; Egis: 31BL;
Hmproudlove: 45TR; Marekp: 45B; Velkol: 49T; Jojobob: 49BL; Kashtan: 48B; Jack Schiffer: 61B; Brigg: 61T;
Steve Byland: 78BR; Eprom: 83BL; Foral: 83BR; Foto280: 99ML; Photojay: 118; Wildcat123: 128; Shur23: 149B
Flickr.com: burge5000: 64L; echoforsberg: 90L; joyork: 98; Liam Daly: 99MR; Jon's pics: 100; The Melancholic
Gardener: 102T; timparkinson: 102L, 114; Jo Jakeman: 106; jhritz: 108T foodistablog: 108M; Dominic's pics: 137TR,
140T; Miss Baker: 140B; jo–h: 144L; moria: 163BL; russelljsmith: 164
Harrod Horticultural: 66
iStockphoto.com: Agmit: 18; David Hills: 30; Blaneyphoto: 36T; Robin702: 42; Imca: 44; Picma: 45TM;
Peter J Seager: 49BR; Charlie Bishop: 50BL; Arlindo71: 64BL; Claylib: 71TR; Vandervelden: 71B; Scarlettsails: 88T;
Gardendata: 90BM; Grandaded: 96; Kgtoh: 97TL; Beagler: 97B; Veter: 99T; Andrew Howe: 119TR;
John Anderson Photo: 119B; MB Photos: 125L; Frogroast: 130T; Blueenayim: 152; Leadinglights: 160
Screwfix: 14

Contents

Introduction 8

Autumn | Winter

Introduction

JUST TEN short years ago allotments were seen as the preserve of old men in flat caps, usually with whippet in tow, who would congregate in tatty sheds to discuss root veg and weedkillers. The flat–cap brigade are still around, but visit your local allotment today and you're just as likely to find students, professional people and young families enthusiastically growing pak choi, mizuna and tamarillos, among the more traditional crops. What's more, many seed suppliers report sales of veg outstripping flowers for the first time in decades, and growing your own is a hot topic everywhere from daytime TV to broadsheet newspapers.

So what's caused this sudden shift in attitudes? The answer is that a number of factors are involved, including: rising concerns over intensive farming practices and the use of agricultural chemicals; a reaction against the supermarket giants that seem to control so much of what we eat; a desire for better–quality,

▼ **You'll find all sorts of clever uses for recycled objects on an allotment. This idea could prevent a nasty injury.**

Safety first

A friend of mine had to take a few weeks off from his hectic gardening schedule after he pulled a muscle in his back while digging out a tree stump (you might think, at over 70 years old, he'd have asked someone else to do it!). It's worth taking the time to do things safely, no matter how fit or capable you are, as a simple mistake can be very dangerous when you're dealing with power tools and garden machinery. 'Don't push yourself too hard' should be the rule. By this I mean don't try to lift too much, don't try to work for too long and, most importantly (at least in my experience), don't try to go too fast! The few times I've injured myself on my allotment have all been when I'm rushing to get a job finished before the light fails or before I have to dash off somewhere else. It's a false economy, of course, because it takes me twice as long to get anything done when I have a bandaged hand or a sore back.

Other risks you might encounter on an allotment include pesticides and other chemicals (if you've yet to come around to the organic approach); sharp tools such as secateurs, machetes and scythes; and the wince-inducing bamboo cane stuck into the ground at eye height – do be sure to cover the tips of these with whatever comes to hand.

better–flavoured food; even a belief that hard times are coming and that we need to be ready to survive more independently 'after the crash'. For many people the motivation is simply relaxation, a chance to bond with family members or to

▶ **Once way out of fashion, 'growing your own' has recently undergone a spectacular revival.**

◀ **Allotments aren't only for veg – you can also grow flowers, and many sites allow tenants to keep chickens.**

spend time away from it all in an increasingly work-dominated society. And for me it's all about the peace and quiet I find on my plot, tucked away in the heart of a city just five minutes from my office.

There are fringe benefits, too – it keeps you fit, puts food on the table, introduces you to new friends and encourages wildlife. Granted, I've 101 other things to do, but that hasn't stopped me applying for a second and third plot, and I'm far from alone in my enthusiasm.

While there are many good books, websites and magazines that concern themselves with sowing, growing and using all kinds of fruit and veg, the aim here is to help out with the more hands-on side of allotment or veg-patch gardening. With just the most basic DIY skills and a few simple tools you can transform your plot into a more productive and money-saving enterprise.

▼ **Allotmenteering is a very practical hobby, but the basic DIY skills are not difficult to acquire.**

If you're a newcomer to the hobby you should start this book at the beginning, where you'll find advice on getting hold of an allotment and running it effectively. Allotments have a culture all of their own, and it can seem like a strange little world to the uninitiated! If you're already set up with a plot then by all means dive straight into the projects in the four chapters, divided up according to the time of year you're most likely to find them useful.

Where to start?

TEMPTING AS it may be to leap in at the deep end, it can be worth doing your research first. While around 9 out of 10 sites in the UK are local-authority-owned and protected by law, the rest are classed as temporary, which means they can easily be closed down. That's not to say it's not worth taking a plot there, but you should be aware you could lose it in the future.

▼ **A typical allotment plan, showing the plots available to prospective new tenants.**

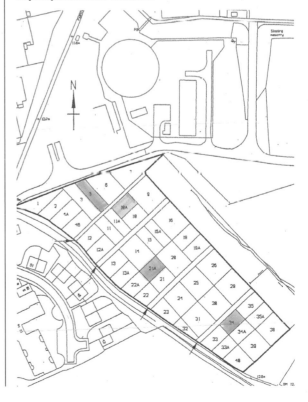

When looking for a plot your first port of call should be your town hall. While they might not own all the allotment sites in your area, they should at least be able to provide you with details of where these are; most will send out a map showing site locations, allowing you to choose the most convenient. Bear in mind that you will need to travel to and from your plot, sometimes with awkward loads. Allotments also differ in the facilities they have to offer: will you need to be able to park; is there mains water or electricity on site?

The final step is the application itself, which these days will most likely involve a waiting list. Don't be disheartened if there are lots of people ahead of you; vacant plots tend to come up in waves when the new year's rent invoices are sent out.

▼ **An empty plot, thoughtfully cleared and mowed by the council, presents many opportunities.**

Getting an allotment quickly

ALLOTMENTS ARE more fashionable in the UK now than ever before, and demand shows no sign of slowing. In some parts of London waiting lists have been closed, while in other major British cities you might face a 10–year wait before you reach the head of the queue. There are still a few parts of the UK, particularly in more rural areas, where space is available. Even here, the more popular sites, those with better facilities, will more than likely be full. Given these obstacles, what can you do to get a plot quickly?

● Although, strictly speaking, councils are obliged to treat all applicants equally, you may find that your chances of getting a plot improve if you get to know the people involved. Find the allotment steward or foreman and make friends with them, and call the people at the council regularly for updates. They don't

▲ **Overgrown areas around the cultivated plots may be up for grabs – if you're prepared to do the work.**

like to see plots abandoned after one year, and if you show you are keen they might see you as a good bet.

● If you are willing to put in the effort, you could even suggest that you take on an area of overgrown land on the outer edge of an allotment site, so bringing it into productive use. This could take you straight past the list of less hardy applicants. A day or two of hard work could provide you with a beautiful plot that you'd have every right to call your own.

● In city centres there are often several allotment sites within a short distance of one another. Why not apply for a place on every single one in your preferred area, then see what you're offered? You can always turn down anything that doesn't suit your needs (although, if you do, you'll have to go back to the bottom of the waiting list of that site).

Did you know?

Under a 1908 Act covering England and Wales, if just six people on the electoral register request allotments where none is available, the local council is obliged to provide them – although this is not the case in Inner London, where there is insufficient land.

Tool box

Keeping an allotment involves all kinds of practical work, and while none of this tends to be beyond the beginner, it's worth buying a decent set of tools to suit the job in hand. You needn't break the bank – £100 should be enough unless you go for power tools – but remember, the cheapest models can sometimes do more harm than good.

GARDENING TOOLS

Digging spade

Digging fork

Hoe

Wheelbarrow

Trowel

Rake

Secateurs / pruning shears

Pruning saw

Watering can

Scythe or slasher

DIY TOOLS

Claw hammer

Club hammer

Screwdrivers

Utility knife

Tape measure

Spirit level

Saw

Pliers

Adjustable spanners and wrenches

Sledgehammer

● You aren't restricted to applying for plots close to home; you could just as reasonably apply for one near to where you work so that you can do the watering before office hours or pick fresh produce in your lunch break. Other locations to consider might be along a convenient bus or train route, near to your child's school or nursery – indeed anywhere within a few minutes' walk of a place you already visit at least once a week. Of course, if you need to drive for miles to get there, you're rather defeating the object of local, environmentally friendly growing.

● Although no legal case has ever been brought to the UK courts, councils do, in fact, have a legal obligation to provide allotment land for anyone who wants it. Why not write to your local authority and ask them what plans they have to meet this obligation, considering the current length of waiting lists in their area?

Tool box

It's perfectly possible to complete most DIY jobs using only hand tools, but if you invest in a couple of power tools you'll be glad of the time and energy they save. For outdoor projects, particularly on an allotment without a power supply, cordless designs are the best option. Top of the list has to be a combination drill/ driver – something you'll find yourself using on almost every project. I'd also recommend a cordless saw to take the effort out of any woodwork. Go for the best models you can afford and remember that the accessories (drill bits and saw blades) limit the performance of the tool, so don't cut corners there.

Jobs to get you started

Join the Club

Some allotment sites hold meetings for their members, but many people in Britain are also part of the National Society of Allotments and Leisure Gardeners (NSALG). Joining this group doesn't cost much and gives you access to free legal protection – not to mention discounted seeds.

Stake Your Claim

If the landowners haven't done so already, it's good site–manners to label your plot to help others (particularly newcomers) to navigate. Some tenants announce their names and even phone numbers, but a simple hand–painted plot number on a piece of wood will do the job.

Meet the Neighbours

One of the best reasons to get an allotment is the sense of community. In my experience new plot–holders are welcomed with open arms – and a few bags of fresh veg. Other allotmenteers are also an excellent source of advice on all things horticultural, so take the time to stop and chat whenever you see a friendly face.

Discover the Lay of the Land

Before you plant anything, work out if your plot has a distinct aspect (i.e. if it faces north, south, east or west). A flat plot without obstacles near by has no dominant aspect, but one on a south–facing slope will be hot and sunny, while ground on the north side of a tall hedge or wall will be cooler and more shady. Understanding the microclimate of your allotment will help you choose what to plant, and where.

Choose Your Plot

If you are very lucky, you will be offered a choice of vacant plots when your application is processed. Pick the one that appeals most to you – but consider the means of access, availability of water and/or power, overshadowing trees and the quality of the soil. Even friendly neighbours and a good view are important concerns.

Late Spring 42

Early Spring

▲ **Make the most of any sunny days in early spring. Getting ahead now will save you work later.**

THIS IS a fine time of year on the allotment and a busy one. Every new sign of life reminds us gardeners that we need to get cracking. It's also the time when many councils wind up the long process of evicting bad tenants, so look out for new faces around your plot and try to make them welcome. A few spare seedlings or the loan of some tools will probably be repaid many times over in surplus veg.

If, on the other hand, you're one of the crop of lucky new allotmenteers, you'll probably be surprised at the atmosphere of community that pervades the hobby. It's a great way to make new friends, and there's no shortage of help and advice – just what a beginner needs. In fact, it can sometimes be difficult to get on with the gardening, but the trick is to carry on working even while you chat. There's plenty to be learned from the 'old hands', including what type of soil you have, what pests and weeds pose a problem and which of the plot-holders have been known to garden in the nude, all of which will help to avoid problems in the future.

Allotment recycling

WE'RE ALL being encouraged to recycle more, and what better place to do this than on the allotment? There's a long tradition of 'make do and mend' surrounding this hobby, and there are plenty of ways we can cut back on what we buy in – so saving money, too.

One of the most popular (and easy) examples of veg-patch recycling has to be the pallet compost bin. Wooden pallets are easy to find, and many distribution companies and warehouses will let you take them away for free. Simply nail or screw four equal-sized ones together in a square and you have your first bin. Fix three more to this, making a double square, and you have a two-bay system, one being filled while the other rots down. The resulting structure is the perfect size for making compost; not so big the compost will be overly compressed yet large enough to get

▲ **The pallet compost bin – every plot should have one. Having three is even better.**

nice and hot, killing weed seeds. You can build as many as your site requires and even add further pallets as insulating lids.

The tops of bamboo canes can cause very nasty injuries if you bend down over your plot without noticing them – easily done if you've just spotted a snail eating your seedlings! A simple idea to prevent eye injuries is to top the canes with empty plastic bottles or those probiotic yoghurt pots, making them both visible and safe. I've also seen old beer cans and even spent shotgun cartridges reused in this way.

Larger projects can really benefit from the recycled approach. Sheds, greenhouses and even polytunnels can often be found second–hand for next to nothing (even free if you can

More ideas for recycling

Large plastic milk bottles Fill them with water and screw on the top, and they make great weights for holding plastic, netting or fleece in place.

Car tyres Not easy to get hold of, but ideal as planters for trees and bushes, or stacked-up three or four high as a 'potato barrel'.

Old tights or stockings Is there any better material for use as tree ties? Soft, stretchy and completely free of charge.

Unwanted or scratched CDs Dangle these from canes or branches to humanely deter birds from attacking your crops.

Toilet rolls Sow your sweetcorn in these, then transfer the whole thing, tube and all, into the ground when the time is right. The card simply rots away.

collect), or failing that can be constructed out of reclaimed materials. Farm auctions and boot fairs are excellent sources of fence panels, doors and old glazing.

▼ **The most efficient way to recycle any material is simply to reuse it in its original form.**

▼ **A little judicious work with a jigsaw and this door fits perfectly into a recycled potting shed.**

Recycled seed trays

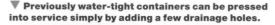
▲ These wooden boxes have far more appeal than any off-the-peg plastic pots or trays.

▼ Previously water-tight containers can be pressed into service simply by adding a few drainage holes.

O NE OF the first jobs of the growing season is to make sure you have everything on hand for sowing and planting. Seed trays and modules are vital for getting your crops off to a good start, but this equipment can be expensive and often doesn't last more than a year or two – the plastic soon becomes brittle if left in a sunny greenhouse. Why not try to recycle shallow wooden or plastic containers, such as fruit boxes from greengrocers, as seed trays?

There are three things to look for when choosing your containers. First, you need something that will be tough enough to stand up to the stresses of the job – strong sunshine, regular watering and being moved from one place to another with a full load of compost. Next, you need to consider drainage. If the container is watertight, simply drill holes every few inches and line with gravel; alternatively, if the container has large gaps in the bottom, as many fruit trays do, simply line with hessian and staple this around the edges. Finally, consider what the container has previously been used for. Did it hold anything that might have left an unhealthy residue? Usually, containers that have come from the food industry are a safe bet, as is untreated timber.

You can also recycle all sorts of other containers to house the plants as they grow. A canny allotmenteer has a good stash of wooden boxes, empty cans or old buckets for just this sort of thing. After all, these look much more cheerful than a line of black plastic pots, and they shouldn't cost you a penny.

Frost protection

ONE OF the gardener's most feared enemies, a hard frost can destroy countless tender veg seedlings and ruin your year's crop of some fruits – but only if you're not prepared for it. In fact, a good spell of cold weather is vital in the battle against many pest species, and can even help to break down your soil by freezing and bursting apart the larger clods. So how do you allow the weather to do its beneficial job in the garden, yet still protect all your hard work?

Cloches and crop tunnels work by creating a warm, sheltered environment and encouraging early growth – several weeks before the rest of the garden. Bell and lantern cloches are for use with individual plants, whereas tunnels can cover a row or more of seedlings. Depending on your crop, you can either sow direct outdoors and cover immediately with the cloche, or you can raise plants in a greenhouse or cold frame and use the cloche when you plant out.

▼ A tunnel can protect a whole row of seedlings or can be used to warm part of a bed before sowing.

▲ Bell and lantern cloches are ideal for dropping over a single tender plant.

Making mini cloches

NO MATTER how obscure a piece of junk might seem, on an allotment someone will always have thought of a way of giving it a new life. This can be true for a large project (my first shed was built using 'For Sale' boards) or on a much smaller scale. It takes a matter of seconds to transform a simple plastic drink bottle into a protective microclimate for your tender seedlings – and, what's more, it's completely free. Unlike larger cloches, these will not need to be removed in dry spells to allow you to water the young plants.

By virtue of their reduced proportions, water will easily seep into the protected area from the surrounding soil. The only drawback is that they don't stay effective for long. As soon as the leaves start to press on the plastic you should take the cloche away, trading up in size if protection is still required. If you don't, the chances of fungal leaf diseases are greatly increased.

▼ **Perfect for individual young plants, these recycled bottle cloches are easy to make and cost nothing.**

1 WASH OUT your empty bottles and strip the labels from the outside. You don't need to be too tidy – just make sure plenty of light can get through. Try not to crush the bottles as you do this, for they might not regain their shape.

2 USING A sharp knife or a pair of scissors, punch through the bottle halfway down and cut evenly around the perimeter so that you are left with two halves, top and bottom. Again, try and keep the plastic in its original condition.

3 THE NEXT step is the most tricky. Using a very sharp knife, punch a hole through the side of each cloche, about 15mm (½in) above the freshly cut edge. The easiest way to achieve this is to make two cuts in the shape of a cross.

4 LASTLY, PLACE the mini cloche in position over the seedling, taking care not to damage the young leaves. To hold it down, push a tent peg (or a piece of wire coat hanger) through the hole in the side of the cloche and into the soil.

Greenhouses

RAISING PLANTS from seed is one of the most exciting aspects of allotmenteering, but I don't know anyone who doesn't struggle to find space for the many trays and pots of compost that are the inevitable result. Warm, bright windowsills are ideal, but few houses have more than half a dozen such spots, and seedlings raised in darker conditions will quickly go leggy. The perfect solution, at least for those with the space, is a greenhouse.

Go to any garden centre or do a quick search on the web and you'll find plenty of beautiful greenhouses, with sparkling new glass and powder-coated aluminium frames – just the sort of thing to make us practical types drool. They are, however, not without a rather shocking price tag – certainly beyond the budget of your average allotmenteer. The answer, as with so many things, is to recycle and make do. Scour the small ads in your local papers for unwanted examples. I have found a home for two in my time, one was free (it needed lots of cleaning and a few new panes of glass) and the other cost £50 but was a good size and had plenty of those all-important vents and louvres. It's amazing what people will give away, so long as you're prepared to dismantle and transport it for them.

▲ Look in the small ads of your local paper and on local websites – you may find someone offering a greenhouse free if you can collect.

As you will be spending lots of time in your new greenhouse, it is a good idea to erect some proper staging. Bending over a low bench will hurt your back, while a cramped, poorly laid-out environment will have you falling over pots and losing vital equipment. Ensure that your set-up allows you space to perform essential maintenance and to stand comfortably.

Despite the extra protection they provide, greenhouses can get extremely chilly during the winter and into early spring. To protect your delicate plants at this time of year, spend a few hours insulating the glass. Extremes of hot and cold can prove fatal both for new and established plants alike, so you may also want to invest in a heater. Use a good thermometer to help you keep an eye on the temperature and adjust the heat accordingly. A warm climate will also allow you to grow a greater range of plants all year round – but remember to open the vents in summer to prevent it becoming too hot. During late spring and summer it will be necessary to provide some shade; try a shading paint that can be removed at the end of the season.

To keep plants moist, even if you go away for the weekend, a self-watering tray is a good investment. The capillary mat in the bottom of this tray allows the roots to draw up only as

▼ Make good use of the floor area and any shelves in a greenhouse – you are likely to need all the space you have.

much water as they need – a healthier alternative to soaking the entire pot. A little liquid feed can also be added to the water to ensure your plants receive vital nutrients. For a more sophisticated system, try an automatic watering kit. As well as saving time, this delivers the correct amount of water in the places it is needed most.

Creating microclimates inside the greenhouse will allow you to grow a much wider variety of plants. A heated propagator is a convenient tool for starting offcuttings and seedlings. You can also add a soil–warming cable or a heating mat to aid the propagation of cuttings and seeds on a greenhouse bench.

▲ Cold frames are a good option if you don't have much space or want to extend your greenhouse.

If you're new to greenhouse gardening, make the most of your opportunities by growing varieties that have previously been out of reach. You can now grow your own melons, aubergines, chillies and bell peppers, as well as propagating bedding plants from late winter onwards.

▼ A good-quality timber design will add a touch of class to a garden or allotment.

Building a potting bench

THE HEART of any serious gardening enterprise has to be a sturdy potting bench, but few of us have the cash to invest in such a luxury, as a good one can set you back £100 or more. It might seem ambitious to build your own, but this is a deceptively simple project for anyone who can use a tape measure, saw and screwdriver.

I've used planed pine for the frame and an offcut of MDF for the work surface, bringing the price of the materials to around £35. This is fine if the bench is to live in a conservatory, shed or greenhouse, but you should opt for pressure-treated timber, which will cost slightly more, if you plan to keep it outdoors. Still, it's not a bad price considering the envy it will inspire among your gardening friends!

Materials and cutting list

Legs: Two 900mm (3ft) and two 1.5m (5ft) lengths of 18 x 70mm (¾ x 2½in) timber

Framework: Six 1.2m (4ft) and six 564mm (2ft) lengths of ¾ x 2½in (18 x 70mm) timber

Worktop: A piece of MDF, plywood or similar, 600mm x 1.236m (2 x 4ft)

Battening: Fourteen 1.2m (4ft) lengths of 20mm (¾in) timber batten

Cross braces: Two 1m (3ft) lengths of 20mm (¾in) timber batten

Shelf: One 1.2m (4ft) length of 140mm (6in) wide timber, MDF or plywood

Screws: 3.5 x 30mm (⅛ x 1¼in) crosshead posi-drive

Tip

If you find the timber splits when you drive in the screws, try drilling pilot holes with a fine drill bit.

1 CREATE AN end panel using one of each leg length, plus two 564mm (2ft) pieces of framework. Make sure the corners are square and leave 18mm (¾in) gaps to fit more framework end–on against the legs (see Step 2). Repeat for the other end, remembering to make a mirror image.

2 JOIN THE two end panels together using five long lengths of framework, one of which goes at the very top of the back legs. This step can be tricky to do on your own, so enlist a friend or try leaning the first panel at an angle so you can rest one end of the framework on the ground.

3 MEASURE HALFWAY along the length of the bench and fix the last two 564mm (2ft) lengths of framework in place, screwing through from the front and back of the frame. These will help to support the middle of the worktop when it's covered in heavy pots, tools and bags of compost.

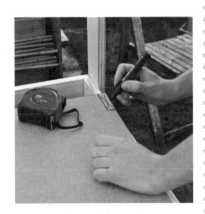

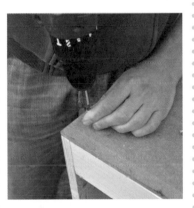

4 CUT THE worktop to size, then mark out and remove two rectangles to allow for the longer legs in the back corners. Worktop materials can be expensive, but offcuts are available from most DIY stores. You could even adjust the bench's dimensions to make use of a particularly good find.

5 IF YOUR work surface is thin enough, screw down through it into the frame in each of the four corners and halfway along the front and back edges. If you're using a thicker material (such as a kitchen worktop) screw up through the frame from underneath or use wood glue.

6 ADD THE last piece of 18 x 70mm (¾ x 2½in) timber to stop things rolling off the back of the top and fix the shelf in place by screwing into each end. Space four pieces of batten up the back and ten along the base (great for storing gloves, tools and pots), then fix the braces diagonally as shown.

Staying healthy

PLANTS HAVE evolved to deal with most of the nasties that attack them, but the allotment, or any fairly intensive regime, is an unnatural environment where many examples of the same plant grow closely together. Furthermore, our food–producing varieties have been artificially selected to give tasty, tender roots, fruits and leaves; it's no surprise that pests appreciate this as much as we do. The breeding process has also been responsible at times for reducing plants' natural resistance.

There are some varieties, however, that are well known for their ability to resist attack, and by choosing these you will stand a better chance of avoiding the problems your neighbours will be moaning about! It's worth bearing in mind that some resistant crops don't produce as well as other types, but that doesn't matter if your potatoes are the only ones on the plot unaffected by blight. Also, you can always put in an extra row or two.

Under glass

IN THE warm environment of the greenhouse, it is easy for pests and diseases to spread. To stop them gaining a foothold, avoid cramming too many plants into the space and regularly check the corners and other hiding places for signs of bugs. Good hygiene is essential – be sure to give the glass and interior a really good clean each year. Seed trays should be washed with a mild disinfectant to eradicate the fungal spores that lead to damping off. If your plants begin to develop powdery mildew or grey mould there is probably poor air circulation in your greenhouse. Clear any over–stocked areas and open the vents regularly. Also, conditions can become very dry during the summer months. This provides the perfect conditions for spider mites. Damping down the floor of the greenhouse will increase humidity and prevent a full–scale infestation.

Top ten resistant crops

Brussels sprout 'Revenge'
Cabbage 'Brigadier'
Carrot 'Flyaway'
Cucumber 'Swing'
Dwarf bean 'Nomad'
Marrow 'Badger Cross'
Pea 'Starlight'
Potato 'Sante'
Runner bean 'Red Rum'
Tomato 'Crystal'

▲ **These tomatoes have been struck by blight, but the peas look healthy so far!**

▼ **Marrows are prone to cucumber mosaic virus, but some varieties show a degree of resistance.**

Jobs for early spring

Grub's Up
Any crop left to overwinter will be ready to race away now that the days are getting longer. Give them the supplies they need by applying an organic, general-purpose fertilizer between the plants and water if the soil is dry.

Hoe Down
Just like your plants, all kinds of weeds will be bursting into life at this time. Act now to cut out a much bigger job later in the year. Run up and down every bed with a hoe, and take the time to dig out larger specimens with a hand fork.

A Quick Fix
Early spring may well be your last chance to finish up any repair jobs on sheds, greenhouses and other structures. Leave them any longer and you'll be too busy with sowing and planting duties to get them done.

Wash and Sow
If you haven't already done so, empty and wash out old seed trays and planting modules for reuse in the greenhouse. It's also a good time to repair any broken glass and give the whole structure a wash down with soapy water.

Feel the Heat
Using fleece to warm the ground is a good way to ensure early crops of potatoes. Buy it off the roll or invest in fleece tunnels. Keep your plants covered until any danger of frost has passed. Hang out the fleece and other materials so they dry in the sun, then roll them up and store away for the autumn.

Screen Stars
Sunflowers make a great temporary hedge for shelter or privacy and will attract beneficial pollinators. You'll get more blooms if you plant them as close as 200mm (8in) apart. Start them off in pots if snails are a problem on your plot, and stake in exposed sites.

Mid-Spring

▲ **The spring allotment is ready to burst into life – and hopefully the gardener is, too!**

F OR ALL my good intentions, I always start a new growing season with the feeling that I haven't quite done enough. No matter how thorough my preparations, the way my plants burst enthusiastically into life never fails to surprise me. From now on it's a constant struggle to keep up with nature, but that's a sure sign your plot is healthy and vibrant.

Once you've decided where your crops are going, you can begin preparing each bed as appropriate. For some it's a question of fertilizing the soil; for others you'll need to warm up the ground to give your seedlings a head start. Some plants, particularly climbers, have more obvious needs, so use your remaining free time to create frames, supports and tunnels where they'll be most appreciated. Unfortunately it's not just your plants that are active this month – garden pests follow the same cycles. The ongoing battle against the slug begins now, whether you're ready for it or not.

Growing ericaceous plants

W E CAN'T all choose what type of soil we end up with, and I've never yet met anyone who considers their plot perfect. That said, there are a few things you can do to sidestep the issues associated with problematic soil. One of the most common hurdles is growing an ericaceous plant, such as a blueberry or a cranberry, in alkaline soil. If you've tried it you'll know the result: sickly plants with yellow–veined leaves (lime–induced chlorosis, to use the technical term). It is possible to change the chemistry of your soil with chemical additives, and a liberal application of organic matter can dilute the problem to an extent. But, if you are only concerned with growing a fruit bush or two, why not get right to the heart of the issue and do away with the original soil? All you need to do is to excavate part of one of your beds and line with a water–permeable geotextile material or a planting bag (both available from garden centres). Fill the hole with ericaceous compost (look for one that is reduced peat or, at least, contains peat from a sustainable resource) and get on with the planting. This may seem like a lot of work, but the resulting healthy plants will be your reward, as will the stares of neighbouring plot–holders as they wonder just how you do it.

▲ A planting bag allows water to pass through but keeps weeds and roots under control.

▼ Blueberries are a nutritious 'superfood', but they don't do well in all soil types.

▼ Filled with ericaceous compost, this bag is ready for a young blueberry bush.

clearing rough ground

BEFORE A new allotment comes up for grabs, it seems to be an unwritten law that the previous tenants will let it go to rack and ruin. The weeds will close in around you as you step on to your new plot, giving even the toughest gardener a feeling of hopelessness. I've heard tell of councils who strim and clear new plots before letting them out, but I can't say I've ever been that lucky. An overgrown plot is no reason to despair, though – in just a few short hours you can transform the thickest jungle into a neatly mown blank canvas.

There is more than one way to clear rough ground, but my method of choice is a combination of hacking back and then starving the weeds. I'm no great fan of noisy engines intruding on my gardening, but having once cleared a large plot by hand I'm prepared to make exceptions. Heavy–duty brushcutters are available for rent from most tool–hire centres for around £35 a day (try for a weekend deal). Look for a model with a metal blade, as a nylon cord will quickly break in brambles and tough stems – but make sure you have safety boots and a face guard.

When the weeds have been thoroughly shredded, you'll need to take precautions to prevent them from quickly springing back up. A sheet of thick black plastic will do the trick; simply lay it over any part of the allotment not destined for immediate cultivation. Damp–proof membrane (DPM) from a builders' merchant costs about £30 for a large roll and is just the job. You'll need to weigh the plastic down thoroughly as it can float away like a sail in a strong wind. Rather than hauling a ton of bricks onto the site, use empty compost bags filled up with damp soil in situ.

▲ A petrol brushcutter makes short work of weeds – but make sure you have the correct protective clothing.

▼ Work up and down the plot, sweeping slowly from side to side – and watch out for wildlife!

▲ For those who prefer to avoid noisy petrol engines, a grass slasher is just the job.

▲ Black plastic kills weeds by cutting out the light. Weigh it down well to stop it taking off!

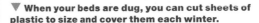

▼ When your beds are dug, you can cut sheets of plastic to size and cover them each winter.

Start small

I still come across plenty of people who say they'd love to give growing veg a go, but just don't know where to start. We've grown so detached from the food we eat that simply sowing a few seeds can seem like a revelation. The only way to overcome this is to give it a go; no matter how little you think you know, you'll probably surprise yourself with the results.

The trick is to start small; don't turn half the garden into a vegetable patch and then give up within a few months because you can't keep up with the weeding. Just grow a few different crops in a small area. Not only will you stay in control of the situation but you'll have more time to notice all the little things that are going on around you. With each passing season the size of your plot can grow with your confidence and experience.

Building raised beds

I'M A great fan of raised beds and tend to treat them as the central part of any allotment plan. The initial work involved in building them might seem intimidating, but it's really not difficult and once completed will cut down on your regular maintenance. There are many advantages to this system: your plot will look ordered and attractive, the soil in your beds can be tailored to your crops and, as they are raised above ground level, you shouldn't have any trouble with excess water.

It's also a very effective way of stopping people from walking on the beds and compacting your vitally important soil structure.

Once your beds are built, dig over the ground inside them thoroughly and then fill with clean topsoil. Mix in manure, leaf mould, compost or sand, according to the requirements of your plants and the quality of the topsoil.

▼ **A well-designed system of raised beds saves the gardener time and effort.**

1 WHEN YOU'VE decided where your beds will go, clear and level the ground as best you can. Mark out the site using pegs and string before taking a step back and thinking about how your plot will work. Walk the paths to make sure you can reach all the cultivated areas.

2 WHEN YOU'RE happy with the layout, measure and mark out your timber. I like to use what we used to call two–by–six (the metric equivalent is 47 x 198mm) tanalized timber, as it's so sturdy and looks great. You can get away with thinner planks, but you'll need more stakes for strength.

3 CUT THE timber to length and screw the sides together in their final positions. There are precious few allotments with electricity on site, but cordless power tools have come a long way in the last few years – well worth the investment.

4 WHEN THE four sides of each bed are in place, cut stakes for each corner and the centre of any long sides. Posts of 47mm (1¾in) are fine, each one perhaps 500mm (20in) long. Hammer the posts into place and screw the sides into them, checking the beds are level as you go.

Keeping pests at bay

WHILE THERE are plenty of animals that should be encouraged to visit your allotment, there are also a few you'll want to keep out. Vegetable gardeners often have to do battle with the neighbourhood cats, who are intent on using the freshly dug soil as a toilet, and allotmenteers might have to contend with anything from rabbits and foxes to badgers and even deer. Whether you're intent on keeping your seedlings safe or protecting your chickens, it's a good idea to get a few defences in place before it's too late.

A solid fence is sometimes an option, particularly with larger pests, but rabbits will quickly burrow underneath if your crops are tempting enough. Such a barrier might also shade your soil, not to mention offering slugs and snails the perfect place to hide. A less obtrusive method is to erect a small electric fence around the boundaries of your plot and, while this might seem drastic, there are now models available to suit just such a situation. You can choose between wires or netting (to keep out smaller pests) and

▲ Cute and cuddly they may be, but rabbits can be a real nuisance if they get on to an allotment.

▼ A simple electric fence is cost effective, easy to install and doesn't do any real harm.

▲ **Connect your electric fence to a car battery. You could even add a solar panel.**

▲ **You can easily find out where snails like to hide and clear them out every few days.**

either run the system all the way around your allotment or just the important areas. If you are lucky enough to have access to mains power you can charge the system from this, but if not there are even solar-powered options.

Having a snail hunt

I GARDEN ORGANICALLY as much as possible, simply because I enjoy the wildlife on my plot as much as the home-grown produce. The artificially comfortable environment of a veg patch can, however, be a haven for snails, and these must be controlled somehow or they will defeat all your attempts at growing your own. Beer traps will make a dent in their population, and barriers such as lava grit or copper tape can protect favourite plants, but in tandem with these techniques I like to take a more direct approach.

On a warm, damp evening a visit to your plot can be something of a horror show with the air filled with the infuriating sounds of snails crunching on tender leaves. This is the time to grab a bucket and start picking the little blighters off the plants, mid-crunch. You'll be amazed at how many you can collect, especially once your eyes become attuned to their colour and shape. Be sure to look in and around old pots and under spreading perennial plants such as herbs.

If you are sufficiently cold hearted, you can then take the snails to a hard surface and squash them under your boot (this is surely a far better end than being poisoned by a slug pellet). If you can't bring yourself to dispatch your charges, then why not throw a few lettuce leaves into the bucket, cover it so the snails can't escape then transport them a good distance away (at least half a mile) and chuck them into a hedge? Probably best to choose a hedge somewhere remote rather than around someone's garden…

▼ **Show no mercy here. Better to squash each and every snail quickly than to have to deal with their countless offspring.**

Building bean supports

THERE ARE many ways to support climbing beans, from the traditional wigwam of bamboo canes to the more unconventional ad–hoc solution. (I have seen old climbing frames and even defrocked mattresses pressed into service.) Many of these allow plenty of space at ground level but encourage congestion closer to the top where the frame elements join up. The technique I like to use (ideal in the space afforded by an allotment) allows you to walk right in underneath the beans and pick them from both sides, which is efficient, healthy for the beans and rather fun for the gardener! Ideally the structure should run from north to south, to allow sunlight to travel down the rows.

Such a sturdy structure might appear permanent, and this hardly fits with a good crop-rotation scheme, but, in fact, the frames are easily disassembled, stored and repositioned for next season's harvest. With just a few screws holding the elements together, it is actually

▲ **Beans are very productive considering the space they occupy – and they look good into the bargain.**

easier to move this timber construction than the equivalent amount of tied–together bamboo. It is also a great way of growing a wide mix of varieties and comparing them like–with–like.

▼ **The trick to keeping beans cropping is to pick them non-stop, even if you have to throw some away.**

1 ALLOW A 500mm (20in) bed for each row of beans, with 300mm (12in) paths in between. Prepare the ground thoroughly, digging over, removing all weeds and adding plenty of well–rotted organic matter.

2 USE 2.4M (8ft) long, 50mm (2in) square posts for the uprights, at each end of the beds and every 1.8m (6ft) in between. Bang them 300mm (12in) into the soil. Link these together horizontally with batten top and bottom.

3 AT BOTH ends of each of the rows, fix two lengths of batten diagonally from the top corners to the opposite bottom corners, to create an X–shape. This will stop the frame blowing over sideways in high winds.

4 TIE LENGTHS of strong string from the top batten to the bottom, spaced according to the planting distances of your beans. Add an extra post to create a 'door' somewhere along the frames so you can get underneath.

Making plant labels

IT'S TAKEN me a long time to learn to label my crops properly – but what a difference it makes! I'm no longer left wondering what it was I planted in that freshly dug bed, and at the end of the season I have a clear reminder of the varieties that have done well and are worth growing again next year.

There are hundreds of ready–made plant labels available from garden centres, and they range in price from a few pence for a bag of 50 plastic tags to several pounds each for fancy slate or metal designs. Allotmenteers have a long history of improvisation, though, and it's a simple job to knock up a few of your own. I've tried various techniques and have settled on two favourites. The first is to cut strips out of a plastic milk carton using scissors – cheap, quick and durable. These are great for labelling the contents of small pots, seed trays and hanging baskets, and you don't mind throwing them away when the seedlings are planted out. For outdoor beds I like to use something much more substantial, so that birds can't pull them out and they can be seen even when your plants are fully grown. A simple timber stake pushed into the ground does the job nicely and can be reused year after year.

▲ This sturdy marker should be much more than a match for an inquisitive crow.

▼ There's no need to buy plastic labels when it's so easy to make your own.

Jobs for mid-spring

Biological Warfare

Being organic doesn't mean you have to let garden nasties have their way with your crops. Biological controls are highly effective and should be ordered now, ready for use later in spring and summer. You might not want to read too much about how they work, as they can be pretty gruesome!

A Warm Reception

If you're anything like me your windowsills at home (and even in the office) are packed with pots and tubs of newly sown seeds. Get ahead of the game by using propagators to bring your plantlets on. Electric models are great; even basic ones can have a fantastic effect.

Feeding Time

Annual vegetables take a lot from the soil, and they're at their hungriest when they're young. You can satisfy some of this demand with fertilizers; I opt for organic chicken manure in pellet form, which is a concentrated nutrient source and very easy to apply.

Room for Growth

If you've planted enough salads in your greenhouse to feed a small army, something I tend to do, now is the time to thin the seedlings. Pinching out a few leaves will not only help lettuces, rocket and spinach to grow back with vigour but you can make a fine salad from the thinnings.

The Last Straw

Make straw paths between your raised beds. Simply pile straw into the gaps between the bed boundaries. It will quickly become compacted, creating a great barrier to weed growth and giving you a firm, clean surface to work from through the summer.

Scare Monger

If you haven't the resources to protect all your seedlings with netting or fleece, take the time to hang bird-scarers around your plot. A few old CDs suspended from bamboo canes will help to keep the pigeons at bay.

Late Spring

AT THIS time of year plants, wildlife and (hopefully) gardeners are bursting with the energy of spring, and with all the sowing, planting out, weeding and watering you'll be lucky if you can find five minutes to take stock. Of course, it's a joy to be outside and longer evenings mean we can make the most of our thriving plots even after a long day at the office, but how do you get to grips with the hundreds of jobs that all need doing right now?

▼ No matter how busy you are, do take the time to walk around other plots; you'll find they're a great source of inspiration.

- To Do -
1) plant out peas
2) Weed herb garden
3) Tie in beans
4) Pinch out tomatoes

▲ On shared allotments a communal seating area is important, as is some means of keeping in touch.

Running a shared allotment

PROBABLY THE two most common things stopping people from running a successful allotment are that they can't get hold of one in the first place, and that when they do the amount of work involved is so daunting that they give up in their first season. A way around both of these obstacles is to take on an allotment with a group of like-minded people rather than all on your own. If you tell your local council you wish to do this they may well push you up the waiting list, as they will be pleasing several people at once. As many hands make light work, you should also be able to cope with even the most unpleasant jobs.

To keep everyone interested and involved it is crucial that you agree what your aims are – what you want to grow and where – and that you keep everyone informed about what's going on. Email and text messaging are both great ways of doing this, but a simple chalk board screwed to the inside of a shed door or left in a greenhouse is a good way of leaving useful notes and details, just in case you keep missing one another.

Another certain route to success is to create an allotment kitchen, with a camping stove and a kettle, so that you and your plot co-holders can relax together and have a chat over a cup of tea and a biscuit.

▼ Taking a few moments for a break allows you to think about long-term allotment plans.

A perennial veg bed

Most VEG–PLOT crops are grown either as annuals, which reach maturity in their first year, or biennials, which put down roots in their first year and then run to seed in their second – although we harvest them before they get that far. This yearly cycle involves sowing, planting and raising a new batch of plants each time, but there are some crops that stay in the ground and are productive from one year to the next. These are known as perennial vegetables, and, while there aren't that many of them to choose from, they allow you to add interest and variety to your harvest without investing much time and effort.

Because they survive the winter and will crop for many years, they generally need only infrequent care after you get them in the ground.

Top five perennial veg

Rhubarb A traditional allotment favourite and rightly so.

Horseradish The roots have a fiery flavour – but watch how they spread.

Globe artichokes They need space to crop well but are worth the commitment.

Sorrel The strong lemony taste makes the leaves very useful in the kitchen.

Asparagus An extravagant delicacy that is easier to grow than you might imagine.

▼ **No allotment is complete without a thriving rhubarb patch.**

▲ They require plenty of room, but globe artichokes have a flavour to die for.

▼ Sorrel is an unusual herb, but very versatile and not difficult to grow.

▲ Horseradish and asparagus, two veg the gourmet chef should never be without.

To avoid disturbing their roots unnecessarily, it's a good idea to group perennials in a single bed where they can have the freedom to grow away. Most have few serious problems with pests or disease, so crop rotation isn't required – there are one or two rhubarb patches on my site that have been there for well over 50 years!

Collecting rainwater

SAVING WATER is a strangely satisfying project, adding a new level to the self–sufficiency of your plot. It's a good way to bring a vital source of water as close as possible to where it's needed, and it's great for the environment as you'll no longer need to rely on a chemically treated mains supply. Any vaguely horizontal surface will make a useful collector, but the roofs of sheds and greenhouses are by far the best, as they tend to stay clean and have a relatively large area. I have also seen people rig up polythene sheeting to catch rain as it falls and even upturned bin lids draining into an old chest freezer (although I

▲ Water butts come in many forms, but aim for as much volume as you can afford.

▼ Guttering makes the most of this shed roof, and the lid will reduce water loss through evaporation.

have no idea how much this would collect!). There are a few simple things to remember to make the initial installation of guttering run smoothly. Before you buy the components from a DIY store or builders' merchant, make sure you have planned out exactly how your system will work. Gutters, downpipes and all the angles, supports and trimmings are far more expensive than they should be, so you'll only want to buy exactly what you need. Take your time when putting the gutter in place; properly fitted it will give you many years of trouble-free service. At each step of the way, don't be frightened to pour water over the roof and into the gutter to check it runs the right way and that there are no leaks. Lastly, don't underestimate the amount of rain that will fall on even a small surface area. A typical shed will keep at least two large water butts filled, which is good news considering the requirements of a decent-sized plot.

▲ Testing guttering is pretty straightforward – make sure the water all flows the right way.

▼ When linking water butts together, be sure to step each one down from the last.

A hard-working crop

ALTHOUGH THIS book isn't about the plants you'll grow on your plot, I'll just mention potatoes here, as they are perfect as a first crop on newly cultivated areas. They are troubled by few pests, need only basic care and will improve your soil by reducing weed growth and breaking up the ground. They are divided into first earlies (planted in early spring – late March in southern England – and harvested three to four months later), second earlies (planted two or three weeks after first earlies and lifted after the same period) and maincrop (planted a couple of weeks after second earlies and harvested anything up to six months

▲ Potatoes are easy to grow and do wonders for the general health of your soil.

▼ Traditionally grown in rows, potatoes benefit from earthing up in their early stages.

▲ When It comes to harvest time, lift one plant gently and see if the tubers are ready.

▼ If you grow your own main-crop potatoes, be aware they can take up quite a lot of space.

later). If you were to grow one of each crop, I'd recommend 'Duke of York', 'Nadine' and, as a maincrop, 'Desiree' for its heavy, tasty yields.

To plant, dig a trench 120mm (5in) deep and line with a little compost or well–rotted manure. The tubers go in with the knobbly rose end upwards at 300mm (12in) spacings in rows 450mm (18in) apart. Fill each trench with soil.

To improve yields, earth up your plants when they're around 200mm (8in) tall by drawing soil from between the rows against the sides of the young shoots. Keep young leaves covered in this way while there's a risk of frost and bury any visible tubers to stop them turning green. The plants will then form extra tubers higher up their stems.

▼ Your crop will store for some weeks in the right conditions, but eat any damaged tubers first.

Making a hanging bird feeder

THE RESULTS of the most recent survey by the British Royal Society for the Protection of Birds make for disturbing reading. The average number of birds per garden in the UK is falling fast. The main cause of this decline is almost certainly habitat loss, as towns sprawl ever outwards and disused land, green public spaces and even our gardens are snapped–up by developers (if ever a profession was misnamed...).

Feeding birds is something many people only associate with autumn and winter, but, with nests to build and young to raise, our garden allies will be very grateful for any help we can give them right now. You should try to maintain a reliable supply of clean water for them in a shallow container – try putting the lid of your water butt on upside down, topping it up from the butt daily. Food is also vital, and you can easily make a simple fatty–treat feeder.

▼ **This helpful little chap will cheerfully dispose of any pests your fork uncovers.**

▲ **A regular and diverse supply of food will keep birds active around your plot.**

Fatty-treat mix

Simply melt down 250g (½lb) of solid fat (lard is ideal) in a pan over a gentle heat. Mix in three mugs of bird seed or peanut pieces, remove from the heat and leave to congeal slightly before applying to the feeder.

1 THE BODY of the feeder is made from a small log, about 50–100mm (2–4in) in diameter and 200–300mm (8–12in) in length. Any left over from heavy pruning or last year's firewood would be fine.

2 USING A 25mm (1in) flat-headed drill bit, make shallow holes at even spacings around and along the log. These don't have to be too neat – rough edges will help to hold the food firmly in place.

3 TWIST A sturdy screw-eye (ideally galvanized or zinc-plated to resist rust) into the very centre of the top end of the log. This can be used to hang the feeder from any suitable branch or feeding station.

4 MAKE A batch of your chosen food mix and scrape into the holes. Wrap the log in cling film and put in the fridge to make it set. When the food is solid, remove the cling film and hang the feeder.

Building compost bins

MAKING GOOD compost is one of the most important techniques in an organic garden. Growing veg is asking quite a lot from your soil, so you need to make sure you give back what you take away. If you have room – and on an allotment you should have – the best method is to use a three-bay bin, which will allow you space to store well-rotted compost, a place to pile up new material through the year and somewhere to leave last year's garden waste to rot down thoroughly. By cycling through the bins you'll never be short of that nutritious, magical end product.

I don't have space at home for such a grand production line, but I make sure I store all my prunings, lawn clippings and kitchen waste ready for a trip to the allotment. Putting such useful stuff in the trash is a terrible waste.

▲ Your compost heap is the engine room of your allotment, so it's worth taking the time to get it right.

▼ Kitchen scraps, garden waste and even shredded cardboard can be recycled in this way.

1 CHOOSE A spot with good access from the rest of the allotment. Remember, you'll make many more trips to the composter than from it, so if your site slopes aim to build it at the lower part of the plot. Rake the soil level as best you can.

2 USING PRESSURE-TREATED timber, build the back wall. It needs to be 3m (10ft) long and around 1m (3ft) high, with posts at 1m (3ft) intervals. I used 150mm (6in) gravel boards and 47mm (2in) posts with a little extra length to push into the ground.

3 USING THE same timber cut to 1m (3ft) lengths, build four walls out from the back wall. This will create three distinct bays that can be used for different stages of composting. Check the walls are level as you go.

4 TO ADD stability, add two crossbars to the top and bottom of the bins. If you want to add a complete front wall, which will insulate and speed composting up, it must be removable to allow wheelbarrow access (see following project).

Making doors for compost bins

THE BIN described in the previous project would work fine on its own, but the addition of doors gives a neater end result and helps to insulate the heap. Keeping the organic waste warm is a crucial part of the process because the bacteria that break it down work best with a little heat. A warm compost bin will work many times faster than one left out in the cold. After the doors have been added, you could even make a cosy insulating blanket out of an old duvet or a large piece of polystyrene.

▼ **This simple 'lid' will keep the heat in and help your compost work faster.**

1 USING THE frame of the compost bin as one side of a channel, screw a length of batten parallel to this to create the second side. The distance between the two sides should be around 6mm (¼in) more than the thickness of the timber used for the door.

2 MEASURE THE distance between the walls of the compost bin at several different heights – if the distance is uniform you can cut all the planks for the door the same length. If it varies, it would be best to try to push the frame of the bin into alignment before you start.

3 MEASURE AND cut the timber to make the planks for the door. You'll get a neater finish if you use the same timber that you used for the rest of the bin. A cordless jigsaw is a useful tool for jobs such as this, and a couple of plastic beer crates are invaluable as trestles.

4 LASTLY, SIMPLY drop the planks into place between the two vertical channels. If they stick, don't try to force them in – just lift the lowest end slightly and they should fall free. When the time comes to empty your bin, you can simply lift out the planks and set aside.

Fitting a solar shed light

As SUMMER approaches it's tempting to stay on the allotment later, making the most of the daylight hours we've been deprived of for so long. Fitting a light in your shed is a great idea if you just can't wait for the lighter evenings, but few allotmenteers are lucky enough to have electricity on their plots. A solar–powered light is the ideal solution, and it couldn't be easier to install. A robust solar panel sits on the roof of your shed, held in place by sticky pads or screws. The light itself is screwed to the inside of the shed and joined to the panel, via a battery, by a single cable. After a short charge it's ready to use and can illuminate your work for many hours.

Solar myths

• It doesn't have to be a sunny day for a solar panel to work – in fact, light cloud is the best weather, as it reflects light on to the panel from all directions.

• Similarly, the light will happily work at night thanks to its rechargeable batteries. It's a good idea to keep the panel clean, though – dirt will block out the sun.

• Some people believe solar energy is a false economy, because the energy used in a panel's construction is more than it will ever produce. This isn't true. Solar panels repay the energy and money invested in them over time.

▲ Fix your panel firmly in place, somewhere difficult for thieves to get at it.

▼ Tack the wire along the frame of your shed and run it through the wall under the eaves.

▲ Make sure the panel isn't overshadowed by buildings or trees – particularly to the south.

▼ A car battery is the perfect way to store the electricity until it's needed.

Jobs for late spring

Take Note

Keeping track of which seed varieties you've planted is easy enough while they're in propagators, but it's harder in the big outdoors. Don't rely solely on labels; opt instead for a well-drawn plan, showing each bed and detailing its contents.

Bug Hunt

Pests become more active as the weather warms up – just like most of us gardeners. It's vital to stay ahead of the game by checking plants regularly at this time of year – leave an infestation for too long and you've no hope of dealing with it. Most pests can simply be squashed as you find them.

Thirsty Work

One of the most difficult jobs on an allotment is keeping everything well watered. This time of year can bring some warm, dry weather – so keep an eye on anything that might suffer in these conditions. Don't overwater, though, or your plants will develop shallow roots and you'll have to water more regularly in the summer.

Border Control

The edges of allotments tend to get neglected, but allotment tenancy agreements generally include a provision for these areas. This usually means it's your responsibility to keep them tidy. Buzz over them with a strimmer every week or two, but leave a few wild corners for insects and small mammals.

Digging In

You might have thought you'd finished digging back in the winter, but if you want a really good crop of strawberries it's a good idea to prepare a bed now. Make sure the soil is thoroughly broken up and work in plenty of well-rotted manure for the best effects.

Late Summer 80

summer

Early Summer

IF YOU'RE not too fussy about keeping your plot boundaries ultra-neat you may well be lucky enough to have wild flowers blooming around you as you garden this month. The insects these attract will help you out by pollinating your crops, so why not reward them by setting aside a small corner as a wildlife area? Most people find they have a disused spot that can quickly be turned into a magnet for frogs, newts, hedgehogs, bees and more – meaning pests are controlled without resorting to slug pellets and toxic bug sprays.

Reducing water use

BRITISH WEATHER is famously unpredictable, and each year it seems some or other part of the UK sees a spell of unseasonably hot, sunny

▲ Your plot should really be starting to shape up now, and faster crops may be ready for harvest.

▼ Watering is an unavoidable chore as the weather warms up. Think of it as a chance to relax and collect your thoughts.

▲ Reduce the watering requirements of thirsty plants like squash by applying a mulch.

conditions at a crucial stage of the growing season. Obviously, our seedlings need regular watering, but a couple of weeks' use can empty the water butts in all but the tiniest of gardens. So what can we do to reduce our requirements and make reserves last longer? One idea is to water last thing at night rather than earlier in the day, so your plants get a good drink while the air is cooler. The problem here is that slugs and snails enjoy damp conditions after dark,

▼ Any organic material can be used, but compost has the advantage of feeding the plants at the same time.

so if you suffer with these pests aim at least to water early in the morning instead of the middle of the day when the sun is at its highest.

A longer-term approach is to encourage your plants to put down deep roots. Water thoroughly but not too often so that roots grow deep to search out fresh supplies for themselves. Avoid watering little and often, as roots will only form close to the surface where they will quickly bake in any unexpected dry spell.

A further measure is to select plant varieties that are known to have resistance to dry conditions. They will usually be listed as drought tolerant and are often bred in drier regions such as those with a Mediterranean-style climate.

Mulch to conserve moisture

ONE EASY way to cut down on your irrigation requirements is to spread a protective layer of mulch around and between your crops so that the soil is shaded and doesn't lose so much moisture through evaporation. There are other benefits, too: weeds will be suppressed, soil warmed up early in the season and even the slugs will be kept at bay if you use something sharp or gritty.

There are many materials available for mulching, from shredded paper or cardboard to specialized heat-reflective matting. I often use shredded bark or wood chippings because they can be dug into the soil and left to rot at the end of the year. They also tend to be rough and spiky so keeping slugs away from tender leaves.

To create a proper weed-proof barrier you should use a light-excluding membrane topped with a good 80–100mm (3–4in) of mulch, but this method is perhaps only suitable for perennial plants or fruit bushes. A thinner layer will also be helpful, provided you kill off as many weeds as you can by hoeing the soil thoroughly beforehand. Anything that grows through this can easily be pulled up.

Another tip to save water is to keep your butts and other reservoirs tightly covered so that when the sun warms them they don't lose moisture through the top.

Planting a herb spiral

A HERB GARDEN has to be pretty near the top of the typical gardener's wish list, but, while most herbs are not difficult to grow, it can be tricky to find a spot in the garden where they can be kept together simply because herbs have a diverse range of requirements. A clever way to create a variety of conditions in a small space is to build a herb spiral – a conical mound of earth planted on all sides from bottom to top.

Mediterranean herbs such as rosemary and thyme like very sunny, well–drained sites and will do best at the top of the spiral in full sun and where the soil is bound to be driest. Herbs that need more moisture will grow better at the bottom of the spiral, with sun lovers like mint facing south and others, including parsley and Good King Henry, on the northern face where the lower light levels will encourage leaf growth.

▼ **With careful planning you can make even a small area of your plot very productive.**

1 USING A centre peg and a length of string, mark out the radius of a circle 1m (3ft) across. Clear any grass and weeds by removing the turf completely, or simply lay a circle of permeable weed-proof membrane.

2 YOU MAY wish to edge your spiral in some way; one idea is to dig a shallow trench and lay bricks at a 45° angle. There's no need for mortar unless you're being extra neat – just bed them into the soil.

3 MOUND UP some topsoil (mixed with grit and/or compost if it is heavy clay or very sandy), firming thoroughly as you go to avoid future movement. It should be about 400mm (16in) high and evenly sloped on all sides.

4 PLANT YOUR herbs as described above and water them generously to get the soil settled around their roots. You could add a centrepiece such as the chimney pot – the perfect place for a drought-tolerant rosemary plant.

Make flowerpot bee nests

WATCHING WILDLIFE certainly makes a trip to your plot more fun. It's also true that native bee species in the UK need all the help they can get right now, with populations in an unexplained free fall.

Installing a bee nest is a quick and easy way to make a difference, and you will be generously repaid when your crops need pollinating. You'll find many types of bee box commercially available, and some are very good, although they aren't generally cheap. You can easily make your own, however, by using an old flowerpot and a few other odds and ends.

► **A bee nest is a simple project, great for getting kids involved with wildlife gardening.**

▼ **Bees are vital to the health of your plot, and it's well worth encouraging them wherever possible.**

1 FOR THE best chance of success the nest should be situated along a linear feature such as a hedgerow or grassy bank, as bees naturally search along the foot of such obstacles for suitable nesting sites. To begin, use a hand trowel to dig a shallow hole 30–50mm (1¼–2in) deep the same diameter as the top of your flowerpot and roughly level at the bottom.

2 STARTING FROM this hole, bury a 300–500mm (12–20in) length of tube so that both ends stick up 20mm (¾in) above the ground. The tube should be around 18mm (just under ¾in) in diameter – a washing-machine outflow pipe would do. This is the bees' entrance tunnel, so if the tube is non-porous be sure to make some drainage holes along its length.

3 MAKE A simple cradle of chicken wire and position it in the bottom of the hole. This will hold the nest above the ground, allowing for ventilation and reducing the chance of a flash flood drowning the nest. Add a large handful or two of dry moss or hamster bedding for the bees to mould into a cosy retreat.

4 FINALLY, PLACE your flowerpot (at least 200mm/8in wide) over the nest and pack soil down around the edges. Cover any drainage holes in the pot with a slate or an old brick and leave undisturbed. After a week or two you may see a few bees coming and going from the exit hole – a sure sign that the nest is in use.

Fruit cages

▲ **This fantastic fruit cage will save its lucky owner from all kinds of pest problems.**

WHILE FEW of us can boast of a garden large enough to grow fruit on any decent scale, an allotment presents the perfect opportunity. A decent-sized plot will give you plenty of space to grow all the veg you could eat and still leave you room for several fruit bushes, and even trees if they're allowed on your site.

There's nothing more satisfying than helping yourself to a few fresh raspberries or currants before you take the fruit home. Unfortunately, like all the tastiest plants, humans aren't the only ones waiting for the crop. Birds will eat the fruit before they've even ripened, so it pays to protect your investment. Fruit cages are becoming increasingly popular and are much easier to build than you might think – the large cage in this project was assembled in just a few hours.

Get the biggest cage you can afford; you'll be glad of the room when you're shopping for plants. Quality is also an issue. Aluminium is cheap, but steel will last longer. Also, while timber frames can look beautiful they are more difficult to construct than metal ones.

1 As with all construction projects, the secret is to get the groundwork right before you start anything else. Most cage designs will allow for a slight change in level, but anything more than a gentle slope will need to be levelled out before you can begin.

2 Construct the roof of the cage first and lay it in position on the ground. This will allow you to mark the exact position of the four corners using bamboo canes or sticks. Move the roof to one side and assemble the corner posts and any other uprights.

3 If the corners are designed to be part buried, dig the holes now. Place the uprights in position and check they are vertical with a spirit level. Lift the roof into position (you'll need help) and fasten the various parts of the frame together securely.

4 Once the frame is complete, and details such as doors are added, you can attach the net. Most cages come with a robust, heavy-duty net for the sides and, to minimize sagging, a lighter grade for the roof. Once that's in place, all that's left to do is to plant your fruit.

Making liquid fertilizer

RECYCLING GREEN waste to make compost is an important part of running an allotment, but you can go one stage further and grow nutrient-rich plants specifically to feed to your crops. One of the most efficient ways to do this is simply to make a sort of 'nutrient tea' by soaking the leaves in a bucket of water. As the leaves rot down they release their goodness into the water, which can then be applied diluted (it's powerful stuff) via the watering can every few weeks. Another approach, shown here, is to soak a few leaves in your water butt and use the water as normal. The key thing is to use your water regularly as the leaves break down so the resulting liquid is not too strong.

1 SPREAD A sheet of porous material such as an old net curtain or a piece of muslin on the ground and cut out a 500mm (20in) square. Don't worry about being too neat here – you won't often see the finished bag.

2 PICK A few handfuls of young leaves from your chosen plant or mixture of plants and pile them loosely in the centre of the square of netting. Gloves will prevent nettle stings and skin irritation.

3 DRAW THE edges of the net over the leaves in a bunch and twist to form a neck. Tie the bag closed using strong twine or string, leaving plenty of extra length to allow you to dangle the bag inside the water butt.

4 USE A large S-hook to hang the bag from the edge of the water butt, or tie the string to a bamboo cane and balance this across the top. The bag should hang 100–150mm (4–6in) above the bottom of the butt.

Jobs for early summer

Contain Yourself

If you're growing any fruit on your allotment it will be time to harvest before you know it. Be prepared, and start collecting jars and bottles now so that you have enough to store your produce when jam–making season comes around.

Cut and Dried

If you've opted for grass paths between your beds, you'll need to keep on top of the mowing through the summer months – remember to use the grass clippings as mulch. Small areas can easily be tackled with a rechargeable strimmer.

Hot Potatoes

Depending on when you planted them, your first early potatoes may be ready around this time. Rather than pull up the whole plant, just probe around the roots with your fingers – if you can feel a few tubers it's worth having a better look.

Party Time

Allotments are friendly places, and there's lots to be gained by exchanging growing tips with your fellow plot–holders. Many sites have a thriving social scene – if yours doesn't, why not get the ball rolling by hosting a barbecue one evening?

Clear Thinking

If you have a wildlife pond on your plot (and you really should, so see page 128) clear out any blanket weed and throw it on the compost heap. It grows quickly at this time of year and can choke your more interesting plants.

Firmly Fixed

Check that trees are still securely staked. Storms can arrive unexpectedly and roots that have been disturbed through movement are unlikely to give rise to healthy plants. While you're at it, think about adding tree guards to protect the bark from rabbits and strimming injuries.

Mid-Summer

WHILE THE more organized allotments will have been productive all year long, this is the time when everything really starts to take off. The word 'glut' was probably invented for the courgette, but there are plenty of other plants giving it their all around now. Of all the jobs on the veg plot, harvesting is the one thing I'll never complain about.

I'm constantly surprised by the sheer quantity of produce I bring home, and I've learned my lesson when it comes to storage. While there are few things (notably onions and garlic) I'd never give away, it's wonderful to share your bounty with friends and family. Plus, you're likely to be repaid with an invite to share the resulting meal. Remember, you'll lose marks if you confess that you've already

taken the very best produce home or that the excess crop was otherwise destined for the compost heap!

Of course, the other advantage to this generosity is that it's the best way to get other people interested in your hobby. When they see the results of your hard work (not to mention your sun–blushed and healthy demeanour) they'll be straight on the phone to the allotment office at the local council.

Sheds and storage

TO MY mind, building a shed is a big priority for any allotmenteer. Smugly dodging the showers while your neighbours get wet is surely reason enough – then, of course, there's the added bonus of having somewhere to store your

▼ **A beautiful plot in full bloom. It's never a chore to go to the allotment at this time of year!**

▲ Even a small shed is a great allotment asset, and if you're organized it should give you plenty of storage.

▲ A good supply of fixings, wire, labels and other hardware takes time to collect.

tools. Avoid the common mistake of assuming you can just pile everything in and close the door – all very well until you need to dig your best secateurs from under the wheelbarrow, workboots and offcuts of timber and chicken wire. Instead, kit out the inside with some simple shelves, hooks and storage spaces. Plan the inside of your shed before you start; think about the tools you'll need to store there and the space they require. A worktop is a very useful feature (look for offcuts in DIY stores or even tips), and old kitchen units are a great way to keep things like plant labels, twisty ties and bottles of fertilizer out of the way. Larger tools such as forks, spades and rakes should be hung up together within

easy reach of the door as you will be using these very often. You can buy packs of screw-in hooks for just this purpose (often coated in durable plastic) but you can make your own using pairs of nails hammered in at just the right height.

Don't position your storage so that the route from the door to the back of the shed is obstructed – sometimes this means shelving just one or two walls rather than all four. Also important is to fix shelf brackets, screw hooks and worktop supports to the structure of the shed (i.e. the upright posts) not just the cladding, which will be much weaker.

▼ Leave space for access down the middle, or you'll have to unpack everything to get to the back.

Build a shed

I'T'S EASY enough to go out and buy a flat–packed shed (I've done so myself more than once), but most are made from pretty cheap materials and don't give you the opportunity to do things exactly how you want. If you build your own, you can make it extra–sturdy to deter vandals, add lots of windows to give you space for germinating seeds, or incorporate a sheltered seating area as I've done here. It's amazing how much more work you get done when you have somewhere to take a break or hide from the weather – rather than calling it a day and heading home for a cup of something warm, you can spend hours longer on your plot without it seeming like hard work.

▲ Every gardener should have a good shed. Stig certainly seems to approve of the seating area!

1 GETTING THE frame right is crucial – the rest will fall into place. Use sturdy fence posts for the uprights, set in quick–drying cement. The roof and floor elements are made from scant, a cheap timber used for general construction. The roof joists are spaced widely (600mm/2ft), while the floor joists, which carry much more weight, are spaced tightly (300mm/3ft). All the timber is pressure treated, and the screws are coated to resist rust.

2 GET THE floor in place before you build the walls. A single sheet of chipboard, Stirling board or plywood is fine if you buy a reasonably heavy grade. I've used feather–edge timber to clad the outside, each piece overlapping the last a bit like fish scales. If you're adding windows, you'll need to add some horizontal frame elements to hold them. Save yourself work by making the top or bottom of the windows line up with the cladding material.

3 SHEDS CAN get very hot in direct sun and cold in winter. If you keep seeds in yours, or if you want a proper retreat from the elements, think about insulating the walls. You can buy rigid sheets of rockwool or similar, which will slot between your frame uprights when cut to size. You must wear gloves for this job – insulation is usually nasty stuff and can make you itch for days. The interior is then clad with chipboard to give a clean finish.

4 IF YOU want to include a seating area, you can create some privacy and shade by adding a trellis screen. I usually make my own, but this time I found a couple of sheets in a DIY store that were half price because the outer edges were broken. Cut to size, they're as good as new. Note that the floor needs to be weatherproof – as it's only a small area I splashed out on a few decking boards, but more scant (if pressure treated) would be just as strong.

5 MORE CHIPBOARD makes the roof, and felt covers this to keep the rain out. This is not an easy job – hammering upside down and trying not to tear the felt – so make things easier by leaving the felt in the sun for a while to make it more flexible. It's also a good idea to rest some spare timber on the felt to hold it down while you fix it, otherwise you'll nail along one edge to find you've pulled too much from the far side!

6 THIS DOOR was bought at a boot fair for £8 – it's for interior use really, but I've treated it with exterior paint and will hope for the best. If it warps too much I'll build a simpler one from exterior-grade timber. I plan to cover the glass in the windows and door with wire mesh to deter vandals, and I'll add guttering along the back edge to feed a water butt. Looks like I'll be finished just in time, judging by those clouds!

Building bench seating

YOU MIGHT think it's an unnecessary luxury, but somewhere clean and comfortable to sit is a very useful addition to your plot. It will allow you to work for longer because you can take decent rest breaks, and it will encourage you to visit more often, knowing that it's not all going to be hard labour! You can either incorporate this into your shed or build it as a stand-alone area, as shown here.

To reduce maintenance, start by laying a weed-proof membrane. Think about the view you'll have when seated – it's nicer to look across your cutting garden than at the back of the compost bins. This project has the added bonus of being a refuge for insects, amphibians and small mammals.

▲ **This simple design could make your plot the social centre of your allotment site!**

1 UNLESS YOU'RE working between boundaries such as raised beds, you'll need to contain the area. Hammer in posts every 2m (6ft), and screw pressure-treated timber to the outside of these to make your boundary.

2 CLEAR THE area of sharp stones, which might puncture the lining, and gently lay the weedproof membrane in place, weighing it down while you adjust it. Where two pieces of material meet, leave at least a 150mm (6in) overlap.

3 To STOP the membrane shifting, hold it in place along the edges with metal pins. You can use cheap tent pegs, but the custom-made ones are more secure and only cost a few pennies extra.

4 SPREAD THE mulch evenly and tread well down. You can use bark (as pictured here), wood chip or any kind of gravel or stone. You need a layer at least 50mm (2in) thick when compacted, to prevent weed regrowth

5 THESE CAGES, known as gabions, cost very little and are perfect for making seating. You can fill them with pebbles, rocks or logs – any of which will create an instant habitat for wildlife on your plot.

6 ONCE THE gabion is assembled, add the filling. Logs and larger rocks can be difficult to stack together neatly, so take your time. Leave the top as level as possible to spread the weight of the seat.

7 THE SEAT is made from three decking boards, available from any DIY store. These are nice and thick, in keeping with the rugged feel of the bench, and they should be pressure treated to avoid rot.

8 To HOLD the decking boards together, use lengths of timber batten screwed across the width of the seat. Turn the seat over and the batten should spread the weight evenly across the gabion below.

Gardening for wildlife

BY SETTING aside a small part of your plot as a dedicated wildlife area you will be providing a home for a wide variety of insects, amphibians and mammals, which will help to control pests and create a healthy, balanced environment.

Once a variety of attractive habitats has been created you'll be amazed at how quickly they are colonized by beneficial species. Frogs, ladybirds, hedgehogs, ground beetles and many others will see your allotment as far superior to your neighbour's, and why would they travel far to feed when they could be munching on the slugs and aphids closer to home? There is really very little to do once the habitats are in place except sit back and watch your guests do their work.

▼ **Don't forget the insects when planning for wildlife. They help pollinate plants and feed larger animals.**

Wildlife areas

• When choosing a spot for your wildlife area, consider how often you will need to disturb the site. Like us, wildlife often look for a quiet corner in which to make their homes.

• Habitat diversity is important if you wish to attract as many species as possible. Try to include at least a log pile, a stack of rough stones and an area of dense vegetation or long grass.

• To make things comfortable for your guests, try to shelter the area from strong winds. Use planting or a simple fence made of pallets where appropriate.

• All creatures are attracted by water, so a small pond is a great idea. If this isn't feasible, you could use a bird bath or even an old washing-up bowl.

• The wildlife area doesn't have to look untidy. You could use it as an excuse to grow some wild flowers or even some native, berry-producing shrubs.

▼ **Frogs and other amphibians are valuable allies in the war against slugs and snails.**

Build a hedgehog box

HEDGEHOGS ARE one of the European gardener's most valuable allies, munching their way through slugs and snails during spring, summer and autumn. They tend to live in cosy burrows (in the colder months they hibernate there). You can really pay them back for all their hard work by building a simple hedgehog box. It should cost just a few pounds to make and take you less than two hours.

1 USING EXTERIOR plywood and pressure-treated batten, make a simple box measuring 540mm (21¼in) long by 290mm (11½in) wide and 310mm (12½in) deep. More batten helps to hold the lid loosely in place. The door is 200mm (7⅞in) wide by 170mm (6¾in) high, and the ventilation hole is just over 30mm (1in) diameter. Two pieces of batten hold the box off the ground.

2 NEXT, MAKE the entrance tunnel from more marine ply fixed with wood glue. It should be 200mm (7⅞in) by 170mm (6¾in) to fit snugly into the door (no glue required here) and 320mm (12½in) long. A single short piece of batten fixed to the underside of the entrance to the tunnel helps lift the entrance off the ground and away from the damp soil.

3 HEDGEHOG NESTS are usually well ventilated, but this artificial one is much less so. Make up for this by adding a length of plastic tubing (water conduit is ideal, as is a washing–machine waste pipe) to allow air to reach the interior of the nest. The pipe should be around 200mm (8in) long and angled downwards to exclude the rain.

4 PUT THE box in place somewhere out of the way and add the lid and entrance tunnel. Cover the whole thing with an offcut of pond liner, roofing felt or thick plastic sheeting. Finally, camouflage the box with dry grass and twigs, leaves or even a mound of soil, leaving only the entrance and vent clear.

Building a bird box

A SIMPLE BIRD box is an easy project even for the least confident DIYer, requiring just a few basic tools and one plank of untreated timber – the best size commonly available is 144mm wide by 18mm thick (5¾in x ¾in), and you'll need about a metre/yard in length.

When choosing a site for your box, don't worry too much about the direction it faces. More important is shelter from strong winds, rain and direct sunlight and inaccessibility to predators such as the neighbourhood cats. Don't be tempted to hang two boxes of the same type close together, as you will be promoting aggressive behaviour between birds. Also, keep boxes and feeders in separate parts of the garden, because feeding birds can be noisy and will disturb the inhabitants of your box.

	200mm	300mm	175mm	175mm	200mm	108mm
144mm	Roof	Back	Front	Side	Side	Base

1 ON YOUR timber plank mark out, in this order from left to right, the roof (200mm/8in), the back (300mm/11¾in), the front (175mm/7in), the sides (one edge 175mm/7in, the other 200mm/ 8in) and the base (108mm/4¼in) of your box.

2 USING A jigsaw with a fine blade, cut the plank into the constituent pieces. Use a piece of coarse sandpaper to remove any rough edges and splinters. Drill two small holes in the base to allow rainwater to drain.

3 USE A hole–cutting drill bit to make a 32mm (1¼in) diameter hole in the front panel then screw all the pieces together. You will probably need to drill holes for the screws to avoid splitting the wood.

4 THE ROOF is the last piece to be added, and, because you are using screws, it is easily removed when you wish to clean out the old nest in winter. The box can be hung by screwing through the back panel.

Jobs for mid-summer

Sowing Circle

Harvesting your crops is enormously satisfying, but don't be distracted from your planting tasks. Keep sowing lettuce, rocket and other salad crops to ensure you have a supply of fresh young leaves for the rest of the summer. These can even be sown between larger, long–term plants.

Harvest Herbs

If you grow herbs on your allotment you can harvest some now and preserve them for use through the winter. Pick the leaves or young stems and either dry them in the airing cupboard or chop and freeze (with a little water) in ice–cube trays.

A Quick Drink

Many gardeners go to great lengths to keep them off their plot, but birds do a lot of good. While they might pull up the odd seedling they also devour slugs, snails and aphids. Encourage them to favour your patch by giving them a constant supply of drinking water in dry spells.

Seek and Destroy

In the UK, cabbage white butterflies can be a problem at this time of year, so pick over your brassicas and squash any caterpillars you find. Your plants should be large enough to resist pigeon attacks now, so pull back any netting and let smaller birds feast on any pests you've missed.

Deal with Ants

Ants are certainly remarkable creatures, but they can cause trouble in a vegetable patch at this time of year. They can attack young seedlings, 'farm' aphids by carrying them from plant to plant (and feeding on the sticky waste they produce) and even bite unprotected feet and legs if you stand on a nest. Watch out for colonies between paving and along the edges of raised beds, turning them over with a fork and allowing the birds to pick up the eggs. If the ants reappear too often you might have to resort to dousing the nests with boiling water.

Late Summer

▲ **The peace and quiet on an allotment is hard to beat. What better way to spend your lunch hour?**

IN LATE summer there can be so much produce to bring in that you might wonder what to do with it all, although I've never had trouble finding happy homes for my surplus. It's a great time to invite friends over for dinner – if you're clever with the menu you can probably claim to have grown everything on the plate!

Don't forget to take notes on the successes and failures you've had his year. When spring comes around you'll be glad you wrote down that variety of pumpkin you couldn't lift into the wheelbarrow and which sweet peas you could smell from six plots away.

There's not much in life I like more than to be out working on my allotment – I even enjoy the heavy digging and the battles with perennial weeds. That said, you should always factor in time for a decent rest, and there's no reason why you shouldn't go prepared for a tea break or even a full-on picnic lunch.

Create an allotment kitchen

ONCE YOUR shed is in place, and before you fill it with lots of old flowerpots and broken lawnmowers, why not think about making room for a small kitchen? I'm not talking granite worktops and dishwashers, but there's nothing to stop you installing a camping stove, a cool box and a few pots and pans. A two–ring burner like the one pictured here costs as little as £30 and will allow you to make anything from a cup of tea to a cooked breakfast without any trouble. Food can be brought along each time or stored on site in rat–proof tins and jars if you want to 'eat out' regularly. Camping shops are a great source of inspiration here – one must–have is washing–up liquid that works in cold water so you can do the dishes under a standpipe!

A couple of safety considerations before you don your apron: be sure to keep anything flammable (garden chemicals, raffia, cans of fuel, etc.) a safe distance away from the stove; if you want to really splash out and install a gas bottle any larger than the portable camping ones, keep it outside the shed in a lockable, well–ventilated compartment and run the gas hose through a hole in the shed wall. Bon appetit!

▲ **You don't have to aim high when it comes to provisions – a drink and a snack is good enough.**

▼ **Of course you may wish to push the boat out with a gas stove – or even a solar-powered fridge!**

Fast-cropping plants

WHILE ALLOTMENTEERING is definitely a lifetime bug for most of us, a little instant gratification can be a good thing, too. There are some crops that can give you a harvest within a few short weeks of sowing, and these are great for filling in gaps between summer and winter crops, taking up ground between larger, slower–growing plants or even keeping kids interested in the hobby.

When it comes to fast results there are a few star performers, including radishes, salad leaves and sprouting seeds. It's possible to encourage others to grow extra quick, however, particularly if you choose the right varieties, and if you're willing to be a little unconventional. Beetroot,

Top five crops for speed

Alfalfa The quintessential sprouting seed, giving tasty shoots in three or four days.
Radishes Pick them small and spicy at four-to-six weeks old; great for kids.
Beetroot Use as baby leaves at two weeks and small roots from six.
Lettuce Cut-and-come-again leaves can be ready in four weeks and keep on cropping.
Carrots Sown shallowly in light soil, baby carrots can be lifted after six weeks.

for example, can be harvested as delicious baby leaves at just a couple of weeks old, then the roots thinned for an early tender crop at six weeks. The remaining plants can be left in for a main crop or pulled gradually to top up your supply. Broad beans, courgettes and others can be bought as plug plants and fed well to drastically reduce growing times, while some baby carrots and lettuces can be ready in six weeks from a direct sowing. There is even a fast–growing variety of broccoli raab called 'cima di rapa' (actually a relative of the turnip rather than a true broccoli), which can crop within 40 days.

▲ Radishes grow quickly, and are the crop traditionally used to encourage budding young gardeners!

▼ Salad plants are ideal for intercropping. They tolerate shade well and can be harvested when young.

▼ A line of beetroot can be thinned-out to provide tasty leaves, with the remaining roots left to grow.

Plant a herb-filled sink

HERBS ARE an excellent subject for a warm, sunny part of the garden and can provide ingredients to transform your cooking pretty much year-round. They take up little space and don't need a lot of attention if you get the basic conditions right. They are also attractive and often highly scented; perfect for a patio or porch where you will regularly brush past them. I like to bring them that much closer to the nose by lifting them off the ground in a container such as an old sink or basin. This also allows you to control soil conditions, which is important because plants such as thyme and rosemary like quite a low-nutrient and freely drained growing medium. Many popular herbs are perennial, which means they will survive for several years if they don't get too cold and damp. A blanket of horticultural fleece should be sufficient protection through most winters.

Some species, such as mint, need to be kept under close control or they will swamp the container. Plant into an individual pot and bury this up to its rim inside the sink, then cut off any expeditionary roots as they try to escape.

▼ **Herbs add so much to a garden, take up very little space and are easy to grow.**

1 OLD 'BUTLER' sinks (like that pictured) are available for £30–50 from reclaim yards or boot fairs. They are very heavy, so don't try to lift one on your own. Get it in position before you fill it up (which will make it heavier) and elevate with bricks and tiles.

2 THERE IS only one drainage hole in a sink, and most herbs prefer freely draining soil. To ensure it doesn't get waterlogged you need to add a good layer of crocks. If these are in short supply you could use gravel or even broken pieces of expanded polystyrene.

3 TO HELP further with drainage, add some sharp sand to your compost. Buy a small bag and mix the materials together thoroughly in the sink. The angular sand particles will break up the clods of compost, allowing water to run through.

4 ADDING THE plants has to be the best part. Pay close attention to the height the plants will be when they mature. It's a good idea to use taller herbs at the back and low–growing or creeping ones at the front and sides.

Building supports for fruit

WHILE SOME councils get a bit sniffy if you plant standard trees on your allotment, well–maintained trained fruit trees can slip under the radar. This provides a great opportunity to add top fruit to your list of home–grown produce. Not only that, mature espaliers can act as ideal windbreaks on exposed sites, protecting tender annual crops from damaging winds. And, if you like to garden in privacy, what better way than to plant a beautiful and productive espalier around your plot?

Construction is both inexpensive and simple compared with most other types of fencing, while maintenance levels aren't much higher. The most skilled task is the selective pruning of the trees themselves, but this is still within the reach of a beginner.

Measurements vary slightly according to the type of fruit, but as a general rule use 1.8m (6ft) posts set 1.8m (6ft) apart. The first wire should be 450mm (17¼in) off the ground, then three more at 300mm (1ft) intervals above that.

▼ **Trained fruit, if well maintained, is allowed on some allotment sites, and is rewarding to grow.**

▲ **Growing fruit can seem daunting, but there's really not much to it.**

1 ALTHOUGH TREATED timber isn't likely to rot, I use Metposts for this kind of project. They are quick to install and remove the need for all that digging. Simply drive them into the ground with a sledgehammer, checking they are straight with every few blows. The timber just drops in and can be bolted firmly in place.

2 SELF-TENSIONING BOLTS are perfect for fixing espalier wires – just drill right through the timber post and add the bolt. Don't over-tighten them at this stage as you'll need to take up the slack in the wire later. Work on one post at a time using the wire (Step 3) to measure the level of the corresponding bolt.

3 GALVANIZED WIRE is best for training your fruit-tree branches, as it looks great and takes much longer to corrode. Pass the end of the wire through the eye of the bolt and wrap it around itself a few times. Do the same at the other end and then tighten the bolts gently to straighten the wire.

Planting 'mobile' trees

WHILE YOU may be growing all sorts of veg, fruit trees offer another dimension to your plot. They are hugely productive, great for wildlife and can be very beautiful – the crab apple pictured here is a fine example.

While top fruit is an exciting and worthwhile addition to any garden, it is forbidden on many allotment sites because of the potential for runaway growth. It's also quite an investment in time and money, considering the short–term nature of many allotment tenancies. A solution to both these problems (providing your local council agrees) is to plant your trees in a hole lined with root–barrier material from garden centres. This will restrict growth (particularly if you buy plants on a dwarfing rootstock) and, combined with a planting bag (also from garden centres), makes the job of digging up and moving the tree much easier and less damaging.

▲ This crab apple, in full flower, is a magnet for beneficial insects such as bees.

▼ Strong supports are crucial to healthy growth. Use two stakes to reduce root disturbance.

1 DIG A square hole the same dimensions as the planting bag and drop the root barrier into place followed by the bag itself. Leave the edges of the bag slightly proud of the ground to stop surface–spreading weed roots.

2 FILL THE bottom of the bag with a 50:50 mix of compost and sterile topsoil (available from garden centres) and plant the tree so the soil mark on the trunk is at ground level. Step back and check the tree is vertical from all directions.

3 BACKFILL THE hole with more of your chosen compost mix, using the heel of your boot to firm the soil down gently around the tree roots as you go. Leave a slight depression in the compost around the trunk to make watering easier and more effective.

4 DRIVE A pair of stakes into the ground either side of the planting bag and fix a length of batten between these. Fasten the tree securely to the batten using a special plant tie or an old pair of tights. Mulch around the trunk with shredded bark, wood chip or old newspaper.

Plant a cutting garden

FOR MANY years I was a die–hard veg gardener. I smiled knowingly to myself as I walked past allotments bordered with lupins and marigolds on the way to my forest of beans and marrows. Imagine the use they could put that ground to if they knew better, I thought. Recently, though, I must confess I have seen the benefit of growing flowers in a bed or two. They look great while they're growing and attract insects and birds to help with the control of pests such as aphids.

This is, in fact, quite a traditional use for an allotment, and as such is written into many tenancy agreements. Some even set out a percentage of ground space that should be used for this purpose, although councils don't tend to enforce this sort of thing provided your plants are consistently well looked after. The older generation of allotmenteers in particular seem to recognize the value of a floral cutting garden, although perhaps this is just because experience has shown them the value of taking a posy home to their loved ones – guaranteed brownie points!

Cutting garden flowers to try

Cornflowers
Pinks
Sweet William
Delphiniums
Sweet peas
Dahlias
Sunflowers
Rudbeckia
Chrysanthemums
Flox
Cardoon
Nerine
Tulips
Canterbury bells
Snapdragon
Verbena bonariensis

▼ Snapdragons, *Verbena bonariensis* and sweet peas are all great plants for wildlife.

▲ With a little careful planning and a good selection of varieties, you need never visit another florist.

◀ Dahlia flowers are expensive to buy, but grow your own and you'll have a free supply for years.

▼ Some flowers, such as this stunning echinacea, can also be used as herbal remedies.

Keeping tools safe

Although I've never found theft too much of a problem, most allotmenteers will have fallen victim at some point. It can be infuriating to discover your favourite fork has disappeared just when you were planning to spend the afternoon turning over a couple of beds. Even the most solidly constructed shed stands little chance against a crowbar, so how do you keep thieves at bay?

One trick that, for me at least, has so far been foolproof is to store tools somewhere very visible but unexpected. If you put up a beautiful shed and secure it with an enormous padlock, it's pretty obvious to passing crooks that there could be something of value inside. Who, on the other hand, would ever bother to look inside somebody else's compost heap? I'm not suggesting you bury your tools in rotten veg every time you head home, but why not build a fake compost bin purely for hiding your tools? All you need to do is nail four pallets together, just as you might for a real composter, then stuff any gaps in the sides with dry grass, old cardboard or whatever comes to hand. Add a lid made from another pallet or timber offcut and sprinkle with more grass and leaves to give an authentic finish. Longer tools can be accommodated by digging a hole in the base of the fake composter and perhaps dropping in an old bin or redundant water butt to keep things dry.

▼ **This pile of old pallets and other junk conceals a spacious tool store.**

Jobs for late summer

Plot-Sitting

If you're going on holiday for longer than a week over the summer, don't forget to ask a friend to take care of your plot in your absence. Watering will be their main job in hot weather, but they can also keep an eye on your shed, pick beans or sweet peas to stop them going to seed and make sure any early signs of pests or disease are dealt with quickly. If your helper isn't already familiar with your plot, take them on a tour before you go – and by all means let them help themselves to any produce as a reward.

Back of the Net

You need to have a little foresight when it comes to protecting any soft fruit on your plot. If you wait until those prize raspberries start to colour up before netting them you will almost certainly lose them to the birds. If you can't afford a fruit cage, a simple technique is to buy a few old net curtains from a charity shop and drape these over cane and bush fruit.

A Summer Coat

Make the most of long summer evenings by giving any wooden furniture, sheds and other structures a coat of timber preservative. It's a quick job and, if done every two or three years, will make your woodwork last decades longer. Even pressure–treated wood is worth including, as the constant action of the weather will slowly reduce the protection offered by the original treatment. There are now several environmentally friendly options – indeed, many of the more toxic products have recently (and quite rightly) been banned in the EU and elsewhere.

Tried and Tested

If you're friendly with your neighbouring plot–holders, this is a great time to find out what has performed well for them. They share your soil and conditions, so it's worth exchanging notes. And they may well let you sample their produce if you offer them a taste of yours.

Taking Stock

Make time now to think about the overall development of your allotment. It will soon be time to order from the autumn fruit–and–veg catalogues, so think about what you'll need and where you'll put it.

Late Autumn 122

Storing root vegetables
Using green manures
Making a wildlife pond
Planting an edible hedge
Testing the soil
Jobs for late autumn

Early Autumn

AUTUMN BRINGS with it a sense that the hard work is over for the year. Your fruit, veg and herbs need gradually less attention, and with a little luck even the weeds are slowly tiring themselves out. With this change comes the opportunity to make a few preparations for the winter and next year's growing season – after all, thinking ahead is one of a gardener's most important jobs. Bright, dry, early–autumn days offer a wonderful opportunity to get started on those tasks that have been pushed down the list through the summer. I like to make sure all my yearly maintenance, from repairing fruit netting and roofing felt to using an eco–preservative on the shed and raised beds, is done well before the winter weather sets in. This way, the structure of your allotment should be in great shape when the new growing season arrives.

Making mushroom logs

THERE'S A bit of a fashion for fungi at the moment, and having grown some last year I know what all the fuss is about. Although they're easy to grow, you can't beat them for kudos at the dinner table, and they don't take up much space on your plot. In fact, they're just the job for filling in awkward, damp and dark spots under a neighbour's tree or behind the shed.

The range of potential varieties has grown tremendously in recent years, and you can now choose between shiitake, pink oyster, white cap and many more. The other decision you'll need

▼ **It's a good idea to have a tidy-up at this time of year, but remember to leave plenty of places for wildlife to spend the winter.**

▲ Home growers can now choose from a good range of mushrooms, supplied as spawn, dowels or inoculated growing medium.

▲ You can raise a good harvest, usually in two or three 'flushes' from a well-maintained kit.

to make is how you want to grow them. You can buy pre-prepared logs, inoculated wooden dowels or bags of spawn. If you want to create your own logs you should choose wood that has been cut recently. You'll need to drill holes and hammer in the dowels or push in the spawn and seal. Either way, the finished article needs to be carefully sited to get the best results: moisture is crucial, although they shouldn't be drowned, and a shady spot is ideal.

If the idea of mushroom logs seems daunting, you could try growing on a slightly smaller scale. Polystyrene boxes laced with white cap spawn are available from any number of DIY stores and garden centres, while many of the varieties mentioned above can be grown in a shed or cool room using straw, tissue paper or even an old paperback book.

▼ If you have space outside you might consider creating a mushroom log pile.

Growing over a shed

▲ **Your shed might be falling to bits, but who cares when it's covered in beautiful roses?**

AN OLD boy who worked a plot at the other end of my last allotment site once told me off because I was growing a grapevine over the roof of my shed. 'You wanna cut that down,' he declared in his Suffolk twang. 'It'll ruin yer felting.' While he may have had a point about the roofing felt, I think the beautiful vine justified the occasional roof–repair job, as did the sparrows that played among the foliage.

A shed can take up quite a large part of an allotment, especially as plot sizes are cut to meet increasing demand, so it seems wise to make use of the vertical space. While this particular grapevine never produced much in the way of edible fruit, there are plenty of plants that would be productive grown in this way, and many that wouldn't but are worth considering for their beauty alone. A few screw–in hooks or eyes and a roll of garden twine are all that is necessary to create supports for climbing plants, and before you know it those characterless timber walls will be covered in vibrant growth.

Top five climbing plants

Grapevine Grown up a shed wall and over a pergola (perhaps above your seating area), grapes can do well in the UK's warming climate.

Honeysuckle A great source of food for bees and nest sites for birds, you can even eat the flowers and berries of some varieties.

Hop Even if you don't fancy making your own beer, hops are beautiful plants, and the young leaves can be eaten cooked or raw.

Kiwi fruit Perhaps surprisingly, kiwis will grow and fruit anywhere that grapes will, although they do need shelter from strong winds.

Rose Fancy a cottage-garden allotment? A climbing rose such as 'Rambling Rector' could be for you. Use the hips in jellies or teas.

▲ Hops are vigorous climbing plants which look great and can be used in home brewing.

▼ Clockwise from top left: rose, klwl fruit plants, grapevine and honeysuckle all make excellent climbers.

Building fleece and netting supports

THERE ARE plenty of tunnels and cloches available to protect a row or two of young seedlings, but why not protect a whole bed in one go? Using the timber edge of a raised bed as a solid base, you can create a pigeon, insect or weatherproof environment with just a few pieces of dowel and some 22mm (7/8in) PTFE water conduit (that bright–blue pipe that you often see road workers laying, digging up or puncturing!), which is available from most DIY outlets. It can be dismantled and packed away when the plants are big enough to look after themselves, and all of the components are reusable – so for an initial outlay of perhaps £25 you can protect your crops for many seasons to come. I owe this idea to the late Geoff Hamilton – a gardener who frequently appeared on British radio and TV – who could usually be relied upon to think of a simple and effective solution to any problem. If you haven't invested in raised beds, don't despair – just make a removable rectangular timber frame to go around the outside of your existing bed.

▼ **Netting alone will protect from pests, but a few supports will give your plants more room to grow.**

1 USING A cordless drill with a 14mm (⁹/₁₆in) flat–headed bit, make a hole 50mm (2in) deep in the timber at each corner of your raised beds. Do the same down each of the long sides of the bed, every metre/yard or so. The holes should be arranged in pairs, on opposite sides of the bed.

2 CUT A length of 14mm (⁹/₁₆in) dowel into pieces about 150mm (6in) long, one for each hole. Using a club hammer, bang the dowels into the holes so the top 100mm (4in) is left protruding. They should fit tightly, but if they don't, just use a dab of wood glue in each hole.

3 SLOT ONE end of your water pipe on to a dowel, then bend the pipe over the bed to the dowel on the opposite side. Adjust the pipe until you are happy with the height (around 600mm/ 2ft is fine for a 1m/3ft wide bed), and then cut the pipe to length with secateurs.

4 CUT FURTHER pieces of pipe to the same length as the first and install them over the bed to make a series of arches. All that's left to do now is cover them with your chosen net or fleece and fix the edges down fast with tent pegs or bricks.

Building a bug hotel

I'T'LL SOON be hibernating season for many insects, and it's only right that we reward them for all their hard work in pollinating our crops and eating pests. I'm a great fan of ready–made bug boxes and have them all over my garden at home, but here on my allotment appearances are less important. I made this simple version from a length of bamboo lawn edging – a boot–fair bargain at just 20p! – and a bundle of dry twigs and stems. I think it adds a certain rustic charm to my wildlife area, and I'll be watching it closely to see if I can spot anyone moving in. Lacewings, ladybirds, hoverflies and solitary bees (many of which are becoming rarer) all appreciate this kind of habitat, and I'd be happy to have more of them around.

▲ **This fantastic bug hotel contains all kinds of habitats for insects, spiders and (hopefully) even lizards or amphibians.**

▼ **They might not look ferocious, but ladybirds and their larvae can munch through a plague of aphids.**

▼ **Hoverflies are great pollinators, and their young are also capable pest predators.**

1 SELECT A good bundle of coarse stems, twigs and dry grass from your compost heap and place these on one end of the bamboo roll. Anything with a hollow core is ideal.

2 ROLL THE bamboo as tightly as you can around the bundle of stems so you have a mixed core of dry vegetation surrounded by several insulating layers of bamboo.

3 USING STRONG twine or garden wire, tie the roll closed in two or three different places. It would be very bad news for the residents if your hotel unravels in the middle of winter!

4 TIE, RATHER than hang, the completed hotel in a place where it will be sheltered from the worst of the winter wind and rain, such as under the eaves of a shed or in dense branches.

Living with rodents

WARM WEATHER often brings with it a swell in pest populations, from greenfly to garden snails. It's not just bugs that can cause problems on allotments, however; rats and mice can dig up peas and beans, raid seed stores and strip crops such as sweetcorn before you're ready to harvest them. Many people wait for the trouble to start and then reach for traps and poison, but I prefer a more gentle approach involving discouraging the rodents from taking up residence anywhere they shouldn't.

Of course, wildlife has as much right to use the land as we do, and I'm always surprised when gardeners are keen to drive out every living thing other than themselves and their plants. I have a brown rat living under an old bath near one of my plots, and at least one family of mice in a ditch at the bottom of another. They do no harm provided I'm sensible, and to be honest I'm happy to have them around. Despite the myths, they actually carry no more diseases than domestic cats and dogs, and by using the following methods I have managed to keep our relationship entirely friendly for years.

▼ **Rats are intelligent, social creatures that don't deserve their negative reputation.**

1 KEEP SEEDS safe – Most of us have a collection of veg seeds that we top up each spring, with any unused packets being stored until next year. This is a goldmine for hungry rodents, especially in winter when their food is thin on the ground. Make sure you keep yours in a safe place or, if it has to stay in the shed, use a sealed metal container such as a cake tin.

2 REMOVE NESTING opportunities – Apart from food (and water, which will be readily available), rodents need somewhere cosy to sleep and breed. Move piles of wood, pots and other debris regularly, fork over compost heaps or drench with water now and then, and avoid keeping sacking, woolly jumpers or other textiles where they can be nibbled and carried off.

3 GROW SEEDLINGS at home – Peas and beans are particularly vulnerable when newly sown, as rodents love to dig them up and eat them. If you have the room, try to grow these crops in a secure greenhouse, cold frame or on a windowsill where they can't be reached. When they are a few weeks old they will be mature enough to be planted out without attracting unwanted attention.

4 SELECT YOUR crops – On a truly rat– and mouse–infested allotment there may be no choice but to remove one or two crops from your growing plan. Sweetcorn is usually the first to be attacked, but even if you grow the seedlings at home your older pea and bean plants may also fall prey. If you can grow these somewhere else then do so – there's no harm in having a couple of veg beds at home as well as on the allotment.

Saving seeds

THE PRACTICE of saving seeds from one crop to start the next is as old as agriculture itself, but is something few modern gardeners attempt. With so many seeds on offer in every garden centre and supermarket it's certainly easy to go out and buy a fresh supply each year. There's nothing wrong with that – indeed, choosing seed for a new season is one of the great pleasures of gardening – but there are still many reasons to preserve the seed of your existing plants.

While collecting and storing seed might seem like unnecessary work, many plants will give you far more seed than you could hope to get in a packet and for almost no financial cost. You'll know exactly how fresh it is, how it has been stored and, if you're an organic gardener, whether it has been chemically treated before or after collection. Here we look at saving tomato seeds.

▼ **Seed of unusual varieties and certain hard-to-grow veg can be expensive, so why not collect your own?**

How to harvest seed

Podded – Produced in neat pods, these are the easiest to harvest. Peas and beans are the obvious candidates in the vegetable garden, but how about collecting poppy seed to top your home-baked bread? Let the pods turn from green to brown, then watch them carefully and pick as they begin to open.

Hand-picked – Plants such as lettuce, fennel and dill produce clusters of seeds in dense spikes or umbels. Others – nasturtiums, for example – produce very few seeds from each flower and as a consequence are the most expensive to buy. Pick the seed daily as it turns brown, using your fingers if the seed is sparse or by shaking the seed head into a paper bag if it is plentiful.

Berries and fruit – This group includes tomatoes, marrows, courgettes, cucumbers and squash as well as peppers, melons and aubergines. Let the fruit get fully ripe before removing and drying the seed. While collecting the seed is easy, it must be carefully dried and stored to ensure it is viable next year.

1 CHOOSE FRUIT from vigorous, healthy plants that have produced a heavy crop. Leave the fruits to ripen fully on the plant before you pick them or bring them indoors and leave to ripen on a sunny windowsill.

2 SLICE EACH tomato in half and scoop out the flesh, then separate the seeds from the rest of the fruit. Some types of tomato can have many seeds, while others (beefsteak varieties in particular) have just two or three.

3 MAKE SURE that all the flesh is removed, although you can allow the gelatinous layer immediately around the seeds to remain. Spread the seeds evenly on a sheet of kitchen paper and place in a dry and airy place.

4 ONCE DRY, transfer the paper into a container and label with the date and contents. Next season, the paper can be torn into small pieces and planted as with bought seed, each piece with a single seed attached.

Ten easily saved seeds

1 **Basil**
2 **Broad bean**
3 **French bean**
4 **Nasturtium** (right)
5 **Onion**
6 **Pea**
7 **Rocket**
8 **Squash** (right)
9 **Sunflower**
10 **Tomato**

Top tips

- Collect seed in dry weather, after midday.
- Use clean implements and containers.
- Washed and recycled spice jars or paper envelopes are ideal.
- Keep plant tags to label stored seeds.
- Add a pinch of dry rice to absorb moisture.
- Store your seed carefully in a dark, cool but frost-free place.
- Use up each batch of your stored seed within one or two years.
- Seed saved from F1 hybrids won't come true to type.

▼ **Collect fresh, healthy vegetables when you want to save their seeds.**

Jobs for early autumn

Winter Coat

A shed is an investment both in terms of time and money. Look after it, and any other timber on your allotment, by treating it all over with an eco-friendly preservative. Check over glazing and roofing felt for rips, holes and loose areas.

Cutting Back

If you are wise enough to have left a wildlife area of brambles and other growth on or near your allotment, tidy it up towards the end of this period. I use sturdy anvil pruners and a machete. Don't cut back too hard, though – many creatures will spend the winter here.

Mix it Up

Compost needs warmth and oxygen to really rot down well, and this may be your last chance to provide both as the weather begins to cool down. You can still be topping the heap up with any vegetation that you dig up or cut back, but make sure you turn the whole pile every week or two with a garden fork to let the air in. If you are organized enough to have several compost bins or one with multiple bays then an easy way to work is simply to fork from one bin to another, shaking the material to loosen it up as you go.

Plan Ahead

Crop rotation is a technique that can seem mysterious and intimidating to newcomers, but there's really nothing to it. This practice takes a little organization on your part, and it's best to start planning next year's crops now while you can still see what's in the ground from last season. The longer you can leave the ground before replanting the same crops the better your chances of success. See page 166 for more on this technique.

Home Sweet Home

Insects are by no means the only creatures that need a cosy abode through the winter. You'll do wonders for the biodiversity and thus the general health of your plot if you install a good variety of amphibian and mammal nest boxes in out-of-the-way places such as the back of the shed or behind compost bins. Frog and toad boxes in particular are a must for pest control. Do your research before placing these boxes, as many have specific requirements concerning the direction they face or the amount of sunlight they receive.

Mid-Autumn

▲ This is an important time on the allotment. The work you do now pays dividends next season.

MOST PEOPLE don't need telling that gardening is basically about growing plants, but gardening on an allotment has a special flavour of its own. Allotmenteers tend to be very practical types, often with a penchant for recycling and reinvention.

Many people make use of their own particular skills on their plots – one of my neighbours is a gas engineer and has created the frame of a huge polytunnel using plastic gas piping. The bright yellow arches have earned his plot the nickname 'McDonald's'. Another friend is a skilled seamstress, and she spends winter evenings sewing insect–proof covers for her crops using old net curtains found in charity shops. She even has a small homemade fruit cage, the sides of which lift up on a drawstring to allow easy access.

If you're inventive you can find plenty of projects to make life easier next season, but first on the list should be preparing the ground. This is the perfect time to dig over a plot, breaking the soil up so that the frost can get deep down into the ground to kill pests and the roots of many weeds. If you start this job early you can do a bed every weekend rather than in one back–breaking effort. New plot-holders would be well advised to enlist the help of friends and family here – the first dig is always the hardest. Alternatively, you may prefer to get your ground in shape the cheat's way by creating a bank of no–dig beds and letting the elements and our old friend the earthworm do all the hard work. Either way, next year's successes depend on a bit of forward thinking, so don't kick off your boots just yet. Autumn is a key time for the preparation of soil in both established beds and virgin ground.

▲ Perhaps not the most subtle approach, but rotovating does get the job done quickly.

▲ A 'dead-man's handle' will cut power to the engine if you let go – so the machine can't run off on its own!

Using a rotovator

OPINION HAS long been divided over the use of rotovators. In one camp are those who believe they save the time and effort wasted on bashing the ground about with a fork. In fervent opposition are those who believe mechanical cultivation actually damages the soil structure, compacting the subsoil and scattering perennial weeds into the bargain. As with many issues, the answer probably lies in a compromise.

I tend to use a rotovator only rarely, on larger areas of land that are already in cultivation, to break up topsoil between seasons. They are certainly less effective when used on virgin earth, simply because the blades don't reach far enough downwards to cultivate the ground fully. Another useful function they perform is to combine compost applied as a top dressing with the soil, further reducing any large material and giving worms a head start. As far as compaction goes, I would avoid the heavier models and only work your plot once rather than crossing back and forth to pulverize the ground.

The problem of perennial weeds is less easy to counter. Chopped into tiny pieces ready to sprout new life and dispersed through a fine and fertile plot, it's easy to imagine you are creating a gardener's nightmare. That said, every allotment I've had has been full of such nasties, and rotovating hasn't worsened the problem – in fact, rotovating the weeds made them easier to pull out afterwards.

▲ The size of the blades (or 'tines') and the weight of the body both affect the depth of cultivation.

▼ One of the difficulties of rotovating is that you have to walk over the freshly-cultivated ground.

Whenever you use equipment on this scale, it is vital that you use the proper protective equipment. Don't pull that starter cord until you're wearing steel toe-capped boots.

Making a leaf-mould bin

WHILE SOME people complain about the mess caused by falling leaves, keen gardeners know a good thing when they see one. Many of the nutrients stored by the trees remain here, locked up until time, the elements and a few million bacteria join forces to set them free. Some people like to add them to their normal compost heap, where they will certainly do a great job of improving the structure. I like to keep them separate, though, letting them rot down on their own to create a truly wonderful growing medium reserved for my favourite and most treasured plants.

Collecting leaves is easy enough in most gardens, although they always seem to come from a neighbour's tree! Rather than complaining about this, I have come to be grateful and even get a buzz out of seeing the piles build up against the fence. If you don't have a garden and your allotment is tree free, you should be able to find a leafy street where you can fill the back of your car. Avoid taking anything from natural woodland, however.

Some people are satisfied with stuffing refuse bags full of leaves and leaving them behind the shed to rot down, but a simple leaf bin will get the bacterial processes started much quicker.

▼ **Garden rubbish, or valuable resource? The results of leaf composting speak for themselves.**

1 A LEAF bin is a simple structure, easily moved, but it doesn't hurt to put it in the right place to start with. It should be out of the way but accessible with a wheelbarrow. Take a little time to clear the area of weeds (you don't want them growing through your compost) and rake it roughly flat.

2 THIS DOESN'T have to be a permanent structure, so use cheap timber posts for the four corners of your bin. Bang them at least 450mm (18in) into the ground so they are sturdy enough to withstand the odd knock. A lump hammer should do the job, but on some soils you may need a sledgehammer.

3 STARTING AT one of the front posts, tack the end of a roll of chicken wire to the wood using wire staples. Unroll the wire around the other three posts, tacking it in place as you go. After the last leg, cut the wire off leaving a couple of extra inches. Don't attach this end to the starting post.

4 CUT OFF or fold back any sharp ends, then tie the loose end of the cage in place using garden wire to form the last side of the square. This will allow you access to the rich leaf mould within, but first you need to collect up the fallen leaves – suddenly it doesn't seem such a chore any more!

Double digging

OPINIONS ARE deeply divided over how soil should be treated over winter. Should you dig it over and leave it exposed? Would you prefer to mulch with a 'lasagne' of compost, cardboard and grass cuttings? Maybe you should just sow it with green manures and fork it over in spring.

I think the answer to this dilemma lies in the condition of the soil. If you've been improving the ground for some time, then green manures will protect what's there with little effort on your part. Soil that has a good basic structure but lacks nutrients could do with more intensive

▲ A well-dug plot will be easier to maintain (thanks to the removal of weeds) and will repay you with healthier, more plentiful produce.

composting such as mulching, but new ground or that which has become tired and compacted through overuse and heavy traffic can sometimes require more drastic treatment. The term double digging refers to the way one layer of topsoil is removed so that the next layer can be broken up. Yes, this work is as hard as it sounds, but with good management it should only be required once in the lifetime of your plot.

1 START BY making a narrow trench along one end of the bed, roughly the width and depth of the head of your spade. Move the soil into a wheelbarrow to be used later.

2 WHEN THE first trench is complete, add a layer of well–rotted compost or manure and use your fork to break up the bottom of the trench and work the compost into the soil.

3 TURN THE second 'row' of soil over into the first trench and break it up thoroughly, removing weeds and stones as you see them. Continue backwards across the bed.

4 WHEN YOU reach the end of the bed you will be left with a final trench and no more ground to turn over. Simply use the soil in the wheelbarrow to fill this, and the job is done.

Creating no-dig beds

WHILE I'M a fan of getting your beds well dug before you plant them up, the concept of digging over the whole plot each autumn isn't one which appeals to many of us. Happily, it isn't as necessary as some would have you believe. The weather, worms and even the roots of your plants all combine to mix up and break down the growing medium very nicely, and it should stay in good condition from one crop to the next provided you take a few precautions.

Perhaps the most important consideration is to mark out and build permanent paths between your beds, so that when you are tending your plot you aren't simultaneously compacting the structure of the soil. Make sure every part of your cultivated ground can be reached from a path – you should never need to step on the beds again.

Dedicated double diggers will rightly point out the benefits their technique has on improving the levels of nutrients in the soil, but why do a job the worms will do for you? When the beds lie empty over winter, cover them in a thick layer of compost, seaweed, manure or whatever is available. Top these with sheets of old cardboard or plastic to stop the rain and wind washing the nutrients away and leave them to break down. In the depths of winter when the frosts are coldest (January in the UK), pull back the covers to let the cold kill any pests and shatter any big lumps of soil.

Some people even plant through holes in the cover, directly into the rich material piled up underneath. This has the added benefit of keeping down weeds, not to mention insulating the ground and by doing so encouraging early growth in the spring.

▶ **A no-dig system can be made up of layers of organic material, spread evenly over the bed. You can even create a base of cardboard or newspaper to reduce weed regrowth.**

▼ **A covering of heavy-duty plastic is a good way to kill weeds through the winter.**

▼ **Cardboard makes a very good mulch over winter, keeping out light and preventing wind and rain from washing goodness from the soil.**

Providing for birds

IF YOUR plot becomes known among the local bird population as a good spot for a meal and a bath, then you can be guaranteed that your pest problems will be lessened as a result. Throughout the spring birds are rearing their broods, so this is also a vital time to provide the harassed parents with a selection of different foods, while during autumn and winter the newly fledged young (and mum and dad) could really do with your help to get through the cold months.

Screw a bracket to your shed wall for a hanging feeder or, better still, why not put up a quick bird table? Many companies offer a range of self-assembly models at very reasonable prices, or you could make your own if you have some spare timber.

The trick to effective feeding is to supply food with both variety and regularity. This means providing several types of food (unsalted peanuts, sunflower seeds and fresh fruit are all good) and keeping the feeders topped up. It is also important to think of the feeding habits of different birds – some like hanging feeders, while others like food

▼ **A steady supply is important when feeding birds, as without this they will quickly start to look elsewhere.**

▲ **Fruit that is passed its best will go down well with many birds, and makes a handy slug trap too!**

scattered on the ground. You can even buy live food such as meal worms, although this is not for the squeamish.

Water is also very important, and a simple upturned water–butt lid will attract all kinds of happy splashing if you keep a couple of inches of water in the bottom. If you have an edge plot with tall trees or fences then it's still not too late to put up a nesting box or two. The more you offer your local birdlife the better the chances they will protect your crops rather than someone else's.

▲ **Watching wildlife has its own reward, and of course a diverse ecosystem is a healthy one.**

▼ **Don't forget to provide something to drink – in both hot and cold weather.**

Watching the weather

AT THIS time of year the weather has a crucial part to play in what you do on your plot. While I'm happy to be outside in the cold, the same can't be said of some young plants, so it pays to keep an eye on the air temperature. You could do this by tuning in to a weather forecast, but it is unlikely to be geographically specific, so it's better to make your own observations with a minimum/maximum thermometer. This simply tells you the extremes of temperature since the device was last reset – great for

figuring out if there was frost in the air at 3am! Mount yours out of direct sunlight and take a reading at the same time each day. Record the figures, and after a while you'll have a useful and permanent record of the conditions.

Another important aspect of the weather is rainfall, and this is very easy to measure, too. If you make your own rain gauge you'll know at a glance how much watering needs to be done – and, as before, your regular readings will build into an ongoing resource.

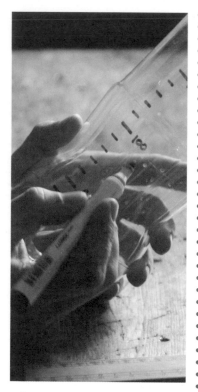  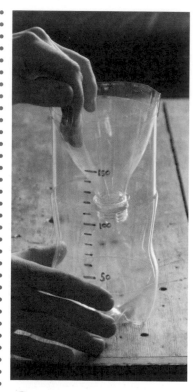

1 TAKE AN empty plastic drinks bottle (1–2l/ 2–4pt/2½–5pt US capacity is perfect for such a task) and, using a permanent marker, draw a depth scale up the side, starting at the base.

2 CAREFULLY CUT around the bottle where it starts to narrow into the neck, then place this upside down, like a funnel, in the lower part of the bottle. This will reduce water loss through evaporation.

3 FIX THE two parts of the bottle together with paper clips (not glue or tape, as you'll need to empty the container) and place the gauge somewhere outdoors where it won't blow over in the wind.

Jobs for mid-autumn

Running Repairs

The elements will soon be closing in, so set aside a good hour to check over your sheds, greenhouses and cold frames to make sure they're up to the job. If they need attention and you don't act now, the winter will soon worsen any damage and possibly affect whatever is supposed to be warm and dry inside.

Plan Ahead

There can be shortage of fresh veg in early spring, so make use of a vacant bed by sowing some texel greens this month. The tasty young growth is great in salads and stir fries. They are ready when they reach about 150mm (6in) in height.

Cold Snap

In many areas the first frosts may appear at this time. Prepare for this by fleecing any tender crops still in the ground or protecting them with cloches.

Start the Rot

If you haven't got one going already, you really should build a compost bin. Any good gardener knows the value of reusing waste material in this way, plus it's free, easy and organic! Let it rot down over the winter, and it could be ready for use in spring.

Try Something New

It's not the first time I've said it, and it won't be the last. Growing unusual veg is one of the most interesting parts of allotment gardening – hey, it's not as though you're short of space. Call in a few catalogues from people like the Real Seed Catalogue, Kore and the Agroforestry Research Trust to see what curiosities they have on offer.

Get Shredding

Composting should be high on your list of jobs now, what with all those annual crops coming to an end and needing to be dug out. Making a really fast and effective heap is a fine art, but you can greatly improve yours simply by getting the contents nicely broken down before you even add them to the pile. A shredder is the best way to reduce garden waste, and electric models are quite reasonably priced. However, if you have a lot of material to get through, consider hiring or even buying a more powerful petrol model.

Late Autumn

▲ **Work on your soil structure can begin as the crops are lifted and cleared away.**

MOST ALLOTMENTEERS spend this time of year battening down the hatches and organizing a (hopefully dignified) retreat from their plots. But, before you head for home, you need to make sure your patch can stand up for itself through the winter. Make any outstanding repairs to sheds, greenhouses and tool stores; small areas of damage will quickly worsen in bad weather. Check that fruit–cage netting, polytunnel plastic and other such materials are tightly fastened down, and store tools away where the rain can't reach them.

The British weather is renowned for being changeable, yet I never fail to be surprised at how fast the nights draw in and how comprehensively the summer is put to flight. One could easily be down in the dumps about this, but planning for the season ahead is a reliable antidote for the gardener's winter blues. Dive into the seed catalogues and make a list as long as your arm (you can always edit it later...), and plan your planting scheme down to the last detail.

There's no reason why you should stick to the conventional when it comes to choosing what to grow. There are lots of companies now that specialize in more unusual plants, so you can plant okra between your tomatoes or medlars next to your plums. It's a good idea to use a few such oddities where you won't begrudge them the space. Part of the joy of having an allotment is discovering new ideas, plants and techniques. As you reach for your new plant catalogues, have a think about what you've yet to discover.

▲ An open structure will provide better shelter from the wind than a closed one, as the air is slowed down rather than simply diverted.

▲ Trees and nearby fences should all help to protect your plot, but you may have to add to these in especially windy locations.

Building windbreaks

ONE OF the few drawbacks of owning an allotment is that, by their nature, they tend to be situated in exposed locations with an open aspect and little shelter from the elements. While us gardeners can nip into the potting shed to warm up every so often, our plants are not so fortunate. Cold winter winds can burn leaves and break branches, setting back growth considerably. While tender and vulnerable crops can benefit from a cosy covering of fleece, it's not practical to wrap up the whole plot. One way of making a big difference with just a little work is to build a windbreak along the edge of your plot, putting a barrier between your crops and the prevailing winter winds.

This doesn't need to be a solid structure – indeed, such a blockage would cause the wind to whip over the top and descend on to your patch in an angry vortex. Instead, you need to filter the wind, breaking it up and diffusing it in the same way groynes disrupt waves along the beach. Woven-willow hurdles are ideal, as their open weave slows the wind rather than blocking it. They can be very expensive, though, and are perhaps only suited to the poshest plots.

A cheaper alternative is to erect a fence of chicken wire and allow nature to take its course. On a typical allotment the fence will soon be covered in brambles and choked with long grass, creating lots of shelter and giving all sorts of creatures a winter home. Cheaper still, how about a pallet fence? The raw materials can be picked up for free if you know where to look.

Before you start building, do some research on where the wind will come from. In most parts of the UK, for example, the prevailing winds are from the south-west, but the coldest and strongest winter gales tend to be north-easterly,

▼ Traditional willow hurdles make a great windbreak, but these don't come cheap.

Storing root vegetables

THERE ARE all sorts of ways to preserve veg, but one of the best if you want to keep your produce in its original state is to make a root cellar. This might sound complicated, but essentially most root veg and many others (leeks, celery, cabbage) need to be kept in a cool and humid place to last through the winter and into the spring. The simplest way to do this is to dig a hole and bury them. The ground stays at a remarkably constant temperature, and the natural moisture in the soil will stop veg from drying out and shrivelling up. The two basic rules are not to let the store get too wet, and to remember where you built it!

The first job is to find a good location. The cellar needs to stay cool, so somewhere shady is best, but, most importantly, the ground must be freely draining, so avoid any low or damp areas. Dig a hole about 600mm (2ft) deep and as large as you need to hold your surplus. If any water starts to pool at the bottom you've chosen the wrong spot – any veg kept here will quickly rot. Line the base with 50–100mm (2–4in) of gravel and then add your harvest (ideally stored in wooden boxes such as those used by greengrocers). Separate layers with planks to allow air to circulate. When the store is two-thirds full, top with a few layers of sacking or old fleece for

▼ **Small quantities of root veg can be cleaned and stored in a box of sand.**

▲ A good way to ensure a constant supply is to choose a mixture of varieties that crop at different times.

▲ Beetroot has a long shelf life, but can also be preserved in sand like carrots.

▼ Roots for keeping should be put into storage as soon as they are lifted, to reduce the chance of rot.

insulation and cover the hole to keep the rain off (an old door is ideal). You can open it when supplies run low.

If you don't have quite so much veg to store, you can recreate the same conditions on a smaller scale. Line an old wooden crate with an inch of dry sand and lay the veg head to tail in rows. Cover with the same amount of sand and repeat until full. Finally, secure the boxes well to prevent rodent intrusion.

Note that you should generally discard (or eat!) any damaged roots that may spoil and spread rot to healthy specimens.

Using green manures

THE EXPRESSION 'green manure' might not sound sexy, but it's actually a very eco-friendly, productive and labour-saving technique – particularly useful for organic gardeners. All that's involved is growing a certain type of plant on vacant ground in your veg patch to improve the soil for the next crop. This can work in a variety of ways. You may remember from school biology lessons that some types of plants 'fix' nitrogen from the atmosphere into the soil. Without getting too technical, this is a really good thing for the next plant that grows in the same spot, because plants feed in part on nitrogen.

Not all green-manure plants are nitrogen fixers; some simply have fast-growing roots that go down deep and bring nutrients up closer to the surface. Dig these plants into the topsoil a few weeks before you wish to reuse the ground, and the nutrients will be released during decomposition. Another advantage of vigorous root systems is that they open the soil up, allowing air and water to permeate. The good news doesn't stop there. Many green manures have dense foliage that covers the surface of the soil, overshadowing and thus slowing down the growth of weeds, and their flowers will attract beneficial insects to pollinate and protect your other crops.

There are many plants suitable for this use. Some are best grown through the summer, but I rarely want to spare them the space when I could be growing edibles. Better in my view to

▼ While the roots of green manures do their underground work, the flowers are great for bees and other insects.

▲ **Alfalfa has deep roots, so does well in dry conditions, and can be sown in autumn and left to overwinter.**

Try these...

'Crimson clover' A good choice for smothering weeds, this is the best variety of clover for planting late in the year. It is not always winter-hardy in colder areas, but where it does make it through to the spring you'll be rewarded with stunning flowers.

Mustard A very quick-growing, short-term manure that is said to reduce wireworm (a pest of potatoes) in the soil. It should be dug in before it blooms, and, if the winter frosts kill the foliage, leave it in place as a protective ground cover.

Phacelia A tough plant that should survive the colder months, phacelia's extensive roots help to break up the soil. Its dense, attractive foliage is good for preventing weed growth, and the flowers are pretty, too.

go for the winter-hardy varieties that will do their job, albeit less quickly, when you don't need the ground for your fruit and veg. All you need to do after collecting your summer harvest is pull up any remaining growth, fork over the soil and sow the green manure. This will grow slowly through winter and burst into life come spring. When you need the ground again you can dig in the manure as you fork over the soil a second time, ready for the new season's crop.

Larger seeds will need to be planted in shallow, closely spaced furrows, while smaller ones can be broadcast sown – in other words sprinkled over the soil – and covered with a light raking.

▼ **Mustard is a very fast crop, and is often seen growing in great swathes on oommercial farms.**

Making a wildlife pond

THE MOST important part of any wildlife garden is a source of water – it will act like a magnet to birds, mammals and amphibians. A couple of frogs or a hedgehog will do more damage to the local slug population than a box of toxic slug pellets, while a few blue tits should keep aphid numbers down.

You can use any waterproof container for your pond, but popular options include old bathtubs or butler sinks. You can also use a flexible pond liner to create a more natural effect – but make sure you don't puncture it in the rough–and–ready environment of the allotment. Simply dig a hole so that your container can be sunk to ground level, seal any plug or drainage holes and fill with water. Add a few plants if you like, choosing a mixture of spreading and upright native forms, and you're away.

Most creatures will be happy using any pool that isn't too green and stagnant – but there are some further rules to making a really good one. First, you must make sure there is a good route into and out of the water, so that anything that falls in can climb out again. A large rock or well–anchored log is ideal; or, if you are using a flexible pond liner, make one edge shallower and cover it with gravel. Also important is that the water should be there all the time, which means either you need to use a deep container that won't dry out or you should be around often enough to top it up. Lastly, leave some long grass or provide a few low–growing plants near by so that the shyer species can reach the water without crossing too much open space.

▼ As soon as your pond is finished, wildlife will begin to arrive. Shallow water is important for many species.

Top tips

• Think carefully about where you want your pond. It might seem obvious, but water runs downhill, so a natural depression is the perfect place to start.

• When you've decided where to site your pond, mark out the boundaries with a length of hosepipe or a line of sand so you know where to dig.

• While a pond liner might not seem natural, it is the best way to ensure your pond stays full. Remove sharp stones (which might pierce the liner) from the bed of the pond. Consider using a protective layer of sand or plastic under the liner.

• Try to create varied habitats within your pond. Deep water is fine, but gently sloping shallows are more important for many birds, mammals and amphibians.

• When planting your pond, look for native plant species, which will be much more appealing to insects than showy exotics. They can still be very attractive.

▲ **Don't forget to add some means of escape if your pond has steep sides.**

▼ **Rare moments such as this make building a pond well worthwhile.**

Pond watching

Once your pond is complete, it will take no time at all for the local wildlife to take an interest. Pond watching is an absorbing pastime and is one of the best ways to get young people to take notice of the world around them. The edges of your pond will be the best place to start looking, and it's worth remembering that early morning and late evening are often the busiest times for birds and mammals.

If watching is not enough, a small net (such as those sold in seaside shops) and a large bowl or jar of water are all you need to start pond dipping. This is a great way to study small insects and amphibians – but an adult should always be on hand, as it's easy to lose your footing when you're concentrating on nabbing a prize bug. Move the net gently through the water, brushing through plants where possible. A healthy pond will probably produce several mini-beasts with each attempt, although many of them will be too tiny to see until you have them up close. Remember that this can be stressful for the wildlife involved. Never leave your catch unattended or in direct sunlight, and be sure to let them go again once you've had a good look.

Planting an edible hedge

ONE OF my favourite tricks is to create a hedge of unusual fruiting plants (sometimes known as a 'fedge') to protect my plot from harsh winter winds. This has the added bonus of being a great habitat for local wildlife and, of course, producing various edible delights.

There are many ways to plant a hedge. Traditional methods involve complex and skilful pruning to get the plants to grow together in a dense block, but I'm no expert, so I tend to content myself with choosing a few likely looking plants and planting them close together in a neat line. Most shrubs and trees can be used, but some will outgrow others, so if you want to keep things in proportion you'll have to cut them back accordingly. One further thing to remember is that these plants need to be pollinated, just like your apples and pears. Do a little research before you start planting to ensure you have at least two examples of anything that isn't self-fertile.

This project depends on one crucial ingredient, car tyres – and these are becoming hard to get hold of. Tyres are classified as controlled waste and must be disposed of in the correct way. I tried three garages, and all of them told me they could get into trouble if they couldn't account for all the old tyres they'd removed. Luckily one of them was prepared to give me four on 'long-term loan'.

I've contacted the UK Environment Agency to check the rules, and they confirmed that nobody would get into trouble for using tyres on an allotment (or supplying them, responsibly, for this use) but also that, as the new owner of four fine radials, I had a 'duty of care' to ensure they were disposed of correctly when they did become redundant. Basically, this means taking them back to a tyre shop and paying a small fee to have them properly disposed of. Fine by me!

Fedge plants

Many shrubby perennials can be used to create a fedge, but here are a few to try.

Blackberries Needing no introduction, blackberries will scramble happily through other plants and offer fruit from late summer through autumn.

Blackthorn The fruit of the blackthorn, sloe berries, are so sharp in flavour as to be almost inedible raw, but they add a delicious twist to gin or vodka and also make a tasty jelly.

Elder The flowers are delightful as a cordial or wine, as are the berries if you can get them before the birds.

Hazel Cobnuts taste amazing fresh off the branch, and many hazel varieties look great, too.

Sea buckthorn The plentiful, bright-orange fruits look great all winter and are packed with vitamins.

Crab apples Very much at home in such a setting, crab apples fruit prolifically, look beautiful in late summer and even help pollinate other apples trees. 'Jown Downie' is my favourite variety.

Rose hips Wild and rambling varieties will climb happily through other plants.

1 First, you'll need to clear the ground as best you can of all weeds, rubbish and any other obstructions. Then level the earth as much as possible before proceeding.

2 Roll out a strip of weed-excluding membrane along the length of the hedge to prevent regrowth and weigh it down with old bricks, bits of timber or whatever comes to hand.

3 Place the car tyres on the membrane at spacings suited to the planting distance of your hedging. Using a sharp knife, cut a cross in the membrane in the middle of each tyre and fold the flaps of fabric under.

4 Plant through the membrane as you normally would. Each tyre will create a favourable microclimate, releasing stored solar energy through cold nights and allowing you to target food and water accurately.

Testing the Soil

GOOD SOIL chemistry is vital to successful gardening, and the typical allotment has had countless owners tampering with it. If you're lucky, you'll inherit a plot that has been greatly improved, but sadly many sites are polluted with rubbish and even toxic chemicals. Autumn is the ideal time to investigate, as you can reach every part of the soil without disturbing your plants. Chemical testing kits are available from most garden centres and are generally very simple to use. These will reveal the pH (acidity or alkalinity) of your soil, vital for determining which plants will grow well. More elaborate kits also test for the essential plant nutrients, allowing you to add the right kind of fertilizer. The official method of testing involves zigzagging across the site, taking a sample every few paces, but so long as you take a mixed sample from several spots you should get an accurate result.

1 ONLY A small quantity of soil is required for accurate testing but, to get a fair reading, mix samples from across the site. If you have a reusable test kit you can take several readings to determine any localized variations.

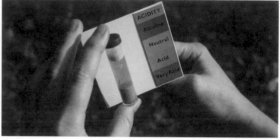

2 CHEMICAL TESTS are the most accurate way to check pH and other aspects of your soil. They are available quite inexpensively, and usually involve mixing a little soil with an indicator solution.

3 THE ONLY way to check soil consistency is by getting your hands dirty. If it feels sticky and moulds easily then the clay content is high – nutrient rich but hard to work. If it feels gritty it contains sand – great for drainage.

4 A PH meter is quick and easy to use. Just push the probe into the soil and leave for a minute or two before taking a reading. They are reusable, but they can be temperamental. Take lots of readings to arrive at an average.

Jobs for late autumn

Swap Shop

Lots of allotment sites have a community building where you can buy cheap tools and materials. Some offer a seed exchange, which is great news for anyone who's managed to save a decent quantity from a favourite crop. You'll need to sign up, list what you've got available and what you'd like to swap it for.

Muck Spreading

Another useful feature of the community shed is that you can often find advertisements there for manure–delivery services. These are often run by local farms or stables and are an excellent way to improve your soil for a small fee. They will bring the muck right to your plot if you have decent access, but be prepared for a tiring afternoon with a wheelbarrow if they have to leave it at the gate.

House Clearance

Greenhouses and cold frames will soon be back in use, so now's the time to give them a good clear out. Remove every trace of last season's plants and wash glass with a mild antibacterial cleaner. Leave windows and doors open so the frost can kill pests.

Stop Thief

As the evenings get darker the temptation for opportunistic thieves to have a rummage through sheds and tool stores increases. Make sure your doors and windows are secure and in a good state of repair – but, most importantly, don't leave anything on the allotment that you couldn't bare to lose.

Collect Cloche Materials

Lots of household waste can be recycled and used for plant protection, so start collecting materials now. An easy tunnel cloche can be made by bending wire coat hangers into small arches and covering these with plastic sheeting. For cold nights, bubble wrap can be added to provide extra insulation. Cut the bottom from plastic drinks bottles to make individual cloches, but remove the lid or make a hole to allow ventilation. While plastic is less efficient than glass in retaining heat, it is by far the cheaper option if you have a large crop to protect.

Starter's Orders

If you have resisted the temptation so far, go through your seed collection and make a list of everything you need for next season. Place your order from suppliers. Most seeds will be dispatched in the spring.

Late Winter 160

Sprouting seeds
Making paths
Crop rotation
Prepare beds for early sowing
Jobs for late winter

Early Winter

WINTER IS a great time to indulge in practical projects. With most of next year's crops still just a temptation in a seed catalogue, there's little to stop you getting a bit of work done on the infrastructure of your patch. While there's a lot to be said for a traditional family Christmas, there also comes a time when it's prudent to disappear for an hour or two, both to work off that second bowl of pudding and to reclaim a little sanity in the fresh air. If you get the weather for it (and in the UK we often seem to on Boxing Day), there's little better in life than turning over an empty veg patch, with your breath freezing around you and the soil bursting into pieces under your boots.

Quite apart from simply enjoying the crisp winter sunshine, there are always jobs to be done on an allotment, and the tasks you get

out of the way now all make time later in the growing season when you'll be grateful for every second you can get. Weeds and pests are about as dormant as they can be, but they are also at their most vulnerable. Frost is a real ally now, and every clod you dig up will reveal tender roots and the larvae of soil–borne pests, while heavy soil itself has no greater enemy than the cold – you can even hear the lumps cracking if you visit your plot on a cold morning. Another worthwhile job is to make a little more growing space. By bringing more of your plot into cultivation in stages rather than all in one go you give yourself the opportunity to stay on top of the workload.

▼ **As winter closes in, plant life slows down. As a result this is a great time to get some practical jobs done.**

▶ At this time of year the value of a shed becomes apparent; it's the perfect place to shelter from passing showers.

▼ If you select the right varieties of some vegetables you can have an ongoing supply late in the season.

▼ As each crop is lifted you'll be able to get started on soil improvement: digging over and adding compost.

cutting back trees

▲ **Tree pruning is not a difficult job, but you do need to invest in a couple of specialized tools.**

ONE OF my favourite spots on any of my three allotments is at the bottom of my second plot, where ordered rows of fruit trees and veg beds give way to a little thicket of hawthorn, brambles and young oak trees. While I could use this ground for a hundred other things, it is a haven for wildlife and provides shelter from the cold north–easterly winds that can ruin a winter allotment.

This doesn't mean there's no maintenance involved, however, and late autumn or early winter is the best time to cut back any neighbouring trees or hedges that are slowly encroaching on your growing area. As they fall dormant for the winter months, these plants are less likely to be permanently affected by pruning, and the cold weather means there is less chance of airborne diseases infecting the fresh cuts.

A badly pruned tree is vulnerable to attack from pests and disease, so follow these instructions each time you remove a branch. The idea is to damage the remaining part of the tree as little as possible.

1 TRIM OFF any side growth from the branch that needs removing. This makes the branch lighter and ensures nearby growth will be spared damage as the dead wood falls.

2 MAKE A shallow cut through the bark around the underside of the target branch roughly 200mm (8in) from the trunk. This will prevent a strip of bark being torn off right down the trunk when the third cut is made.

3 CUT THROUGH the branch 300mm (1ft) from the trunk, supporting it as best you can and slowly letting it fall. You may need help here, as the branch could be heavier than it looks.

4 CUT OFF the remaining stump (making sure it is supported with your spare hand) without damaging the 'collar' of wood that surrounds where it joins the trunk. This collar holds regenerative cells that will help the wound heal.

Draining damp ground

WATER IS pretty fundamental to a successful allotment, but having too much is almost as bad as having too little. Soggy ground is a nightmare to work, and many plants will be sickly and prone to disease in such conditions, if they grow at all. A proper solution to the problem will involve plenty of hard work, but it only needs to be done once. The technique of building a drain is a very old one. It involves providing a quick–draining channel to allow the water to move on rather than sitting in one spot. The problem is that in order to be able to cultivate the ground above you need to dig down a long way.

▲ Sloping ground is often freely draining, but of course somebody will end up with the damp plot at the bottom!

▼ Don't let a valuable part of your allotment fall into disuse; a few hours work can improve it.

1 THE FIRST step is to decide where the new drain will run. Follow the natural fall of the land and use any existing depressions so you don't have to dig quite so deep. A spirit level is invaluable here – you'll kick yourself if your drain runs the wrong way!

2 NOW FOR the hard part. The drain needs to be deep to allow for the ground above it to be cultivated, so you might have to dig as much as 1m (3ft) down. If the ground is very wet this can be backbreaking work – I had to dig this ditch on one day and install the drain the next.

3 LINE THE base of the trench with gravel or rubble, about 50mm (2in) deep. On top of this, place a perforated plastic pipe (available from builders' merchants, although you may need to drill the holes yourself). Check the fall of the pipe with a spirit level and correct as necessary.

4 ADD ANOTHER 200mm (8in) of gravel on top of the pipe and cover with geotextile matting to keep the drain clear of roots. Backfill the trench with topsoil and firm down. Water will obviously collect at the lowest end of the pipe, so you'll need to run the drain to a disused part of the garden.

Growing in damp ground

ALLOTMENTS ARE, by their nature, the leftover pieces of ground that nobody could think of a better use for. They are often unsuitable for building, and a common problem is that large areas of the site are poorly drained, which has obvious effects on what you can grow.

Poor drainage is likely to be worst in the lowest part of your allotment, so why not reserve that spot for the plants that will thrive in such conditions? Some plants will be at home in quite heavily waterlogged soil, while others like constantly moist but well–drained growing conditions. In the worst situations, a good trick is to elevate the growing medium by building a raised bed. This will then drain freely but has the advantage of staying damp, sucking the moisture from the ground below. You will have to accept the fact that even pressure–treated timber won't last so long in these conditions.

▼ **Pumpkins are thirsty plants, so cut down on your watering obligations by siting them in a damp spot.**

Top five damp-loving edibles

Cranberry With legendary health-giving properties and packed full of taste, cranberries are bog plants that thrive in damp conditions.

Horseradish You haven't tasted horseradish until you've grown and grated your own. Divide the roots each year, eat one half and replant the other.

Celery The wild version, introduced by the Romans, is still a common sight by streams and rivers. Modern strains still like to have damp roots.

Pumpkins Liking moist but not waterlogged soil, pumpkins will do well in a raised bed built on wet ground and filled with well-rotted manure.

Arrowhead Not common on the supermarket shelves, but this UK native is farmed in China for its delicious tubers; find it in the pond-plant section of a garden centre.

▲ If your ground is damp but reasonably well-draining, celery and horseradish should both do well.

▼ There are many varieties of Arrowroot around the world, all with edible tubers. Perfect for really wet spots.

▼ Cranberries are a nutritional super-food, and will do best in damp ground.

Storing bamboo canes

ALTHOUGH THEY'RE in use for much of the summer – often for beans – bamboo supports tend to be pulled up and dismantled in autumn to make way for a winter crop that will make good use of the nitrogen–rich soil created by the beans. This can leave you with an untidy pile of sticks that do nothing but get in your way – unless you store them properly. It can be tempting to shove them down the back of the shed, where at least they'll be out of sight, but by next spring you can bet they'll be hopelessly entangled with weeds – not to mention home to slugs and snails.

Despite their awkward proportions, building a tidy store for your canes is very easy and will give your plot a professional air. The store can be built against any vertical surface, such as the side of your shed or along a fence. Remember, you'll need enough space to hang a 2.5m (8ft) cane, but don't space the two ends so far apart that shorter canes drop through the middle.

▼ **Bamboo canes are very useful through the summer, but how to keep them out of the way in winter?**

▲ **Stored out of the way and up off the damp ground, these canes should be in good condition for next season.**

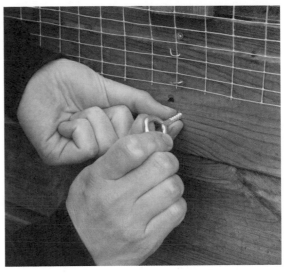

1 FIND TWO strong anchoring points about 1.2m (4ft) apart in the supporting surface, at something like chest height. The upright posts inside a shed wall are ideal. Make sure the points are level, then use a brad awl or a drill to make pilot holes in the wood.

2 WIND TWO strong screw eyes into the pilot holes. If you find them difficult to turn, pass a screwdriver through the eye and twist this – the extra leverage will make the job easy. Ideally, the eyes should be galvanized to resist rust, but plastic–coated or stainless–steel ones will do.

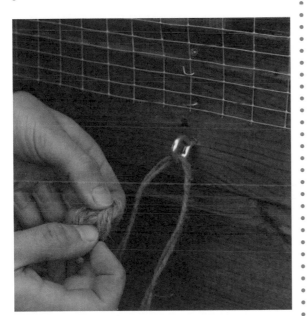

3 CUT A 1m (3ft) length of rope or strong string and pass one end through the first screw eye. Tie the two ends of the rope together to form a loop that hangs about halfway to the ground. Repeat for the second screw eye, so you end up with two loops of rope hanging at equal heights.

4 WHEN THE time comes to dismantle your bean frames, wipe them down with a rag and slide them into the two loops of rope. Here they will stay until you're ready to use them again. Stored in this way over the winter they will also act as a cosy nest for hibernating ladybirds and lacewings.

Maintaining your tools

FARM WORKERS and gardeners of old knew full well the benefits of keeping their tools in good condition, and clean tools were said to be worth an extra man. In our throwaway society it's as easy to buy a new spade every so often as it is to ensure yours remains clean and rust free. However, if you prefer to invest in decent equipment, it's definitely worth keeping it maintained. This is a quick job if you stay on top of it, and it has many advantages. Obviously, your tools will last longer if you look after them, but they will also be much easier to use if you're not carrying the extra weight of dried–on mud. For fruit gardeners it is especially important to keep pruning tools clean; there's no surer way to spread disease than to pass from plant to plant without cleaning the implements used to do the cutting.

▼ **Clean tools kept in an accessible place are far more useful than dirty ones flung to the back of the shed.**

Sharpening spades and hoes

Keeping spades, hoes and cutting tools clean and sharp is a quick and easy job. A sharp spade will cut through thick roots and heavy soil with near surgical precision, while a blunt one will force you to stamp and hack until you're tired and sore. The easiest way of sharpening tools is to use a bench grinder. You don't have to be a craftsman to use one of these, but you do have to be a bit careful. Always wear eye protection and strong gloves while using the grinder, and don't put too much pressure on the wheel (it should run at close to full speed even when in contact with a tool). Apart from those precautions, there's not much to it; just hold the tool lightly against the rotating wheel until the desired edge is created.

1 THE FIRST step is to gather together a small maintenance kit consisting of a cleaning rag or brush, sharpening stones or files and a can of WD–40 or similar lubricant spray. With these stored somewhere ready to hand you'll be much more likely to remember to use them.

2 YOU SHOULD be sure to knock mud from your spade, fork or trowel after each use so they don't rust. Every month or so it's a good idea to give them a really good clean up. Secateurs should be washed after each use to avoid the spread of disease.

3 SOME TOOLS can benefit from sharpening. Secateurs obviously need to have a razor edge, but a hoe and even a spade will be much easier to use if they are sharp. Clean off rust with wire wool before honing the edges with a whet stone, reaper file or bench grinder (see box).

4 IF YOU are putting a tool away for a little while, or if it has any moving parts, an even spray with a lubricant oil is a wise move. Not only will this keep the item moving freely, it will prevent airborne moisture causing rust while the tool is out of use.

Planning your plot

MANY COUNCILS complete the long process of evicting bad allotment tenants in early winter, so, if you're just starting, you may find yourself with a new plot at the 'unfriendly' end of the growing season. There's no reason to be frustrated – just get on with planning it all out!

A landscape designer once told me that before setting fork to soil you should always spend a full year 'experiencing' a new plot. While he had a point in that conditions change through the seasons, I don't think I've ever met a gardener who could restrain themselves for that long. Most of us can grasp the idea that shadows lengthen, weather worsens and garden activity slows in the winter – we just need to use our common sense.

Start by making a record of what you already have – measure the plot thoroughly and draw up a simple plan. Mark the position of any permanent features (buildings, trees, water supply) and, when you're satisfied, photocopy

the drawing a few times so you can work on the design. When planning the layout of your allotment there are a few core principles to remember. The most obvious is to work with the aspect of the site, so give the most favourable (i.e. sunny and sheltered) spots to the plants, while the shed, compost heap and water butt can be slotted into any patches of shade (and will cast their own). Beds should run north to south in order to allow light along their length. Good access to all the beds is also vital and should be plenty wide enough to allow the passage of a wheelbarrow. Think about how the site will work and how much storage you'll need? If the site slopes, will you be going up or downhill with that full watering can? Can you comfortably reach every part of the cultivated ground? When you know what you want, mark out the plot using stakes and let the real work begin.

▼ Get the basic down on paper – shed, compost, beds – and don't be afraid to move things around.

▼ A surveyors' tape measure will help you get to grips with planning a larger plot.

Jobs for early winter

Name Calling

Once you've chosen and ordered your seed for next year, get ahead of yourself by writing a label for each variety. Keeping track of the performance of your crops is an important technique and can easily be forgotten in the annual spring rush.

Net Gains

You might expect most garden pests to be hibernating now, but birds can still be a real pain. Protect young seedlings from peckish pigeons by building a simple frame of canes and covering with bird netting.

Break It Down

If you have large areas of ground in cultivation, you may choose to loosen the soil with a rotovator. This should leave the earth as a fine tilth and can save hours of tedious digging.

Offer Support

If you have fruit trees, it is important to check that they are properly anchored. At this time of year they will be susceptible to wind rock, so ensure supports are sturdy while you're completing your winter pruning. Open-grown apple and pear trees should have congested shoots removed to promote new growth. A well-shaped and maintained specimen is likely to have greater stability to withstand winter winds. While it is important that trees are secure, they should not be under pressure – check that they are not being pulled or pinched by ties.

House Clearance

Because of climate change many British birds are nesting earlier, so it pays to prepare their lodgings before spring. Remove last years' material and scrub with warm, soapy water to eradicate sources of infection. It's a good idea to wear gloves and wash your hands well, as old nests can harbour parasites. During the winter, birds will often use boxes for roosting, so it is worth cleaning them before the weather gets too cold. Adding a small amount of seed to their lodgings will provide an unexpected treat, but don't forget to keep your hanging feeders topped up.

Mid-Winter

▲ **A good sharp frost is just the job for breaking up soil and killing pests.**

THERE ARE still people who don't understand the attraction of allotment gardening, and one of their usual objections is that 'we only get three days of good weather a year'. I suspect such people will never be persuaded to give allotmenteering a try – in my view the UK has the most wonderful climate, full of interest in every season. I certainly don't let a little thing like the onset of winter keep me indoors! As the old saying goes, there's no such thing as bad weather – only bad clothing.

Choosing the right clothes

GETTING PROPERLY kitted out doesn't have to be an expensive exercise – you're going to be working in fairly rough conditions, so there's no point buying expensive brands. I can't think of any part of my allotment wardrobe that cost more than £15 – thanks to car boot sales, charity shops and army–surplus stores.

Starting with the extremities, waterproof boots are an obvious must have – if you let your feet get wet you'll be heading miserably for home. Don't forget that few boots are well insulated, so have a thick pair of outer socks that you keep with them. Likewise, if you buy a pair of slightly oversized gardening gloves, you can wear a warm, fleecy pair of normal gloves underneath. When it comes to legwear, look for some tough waterproofs that will fit over your normal clothes or scour the charity shops for second–hand snow trousers, which should be both warm and water resistant. Your upper body should be dressed

▲ Good strong boots are top of the gardener's wish list
– add insulation with an extra pair of socks.

▲ Fingers get cold quickly, so double-up on gloves.
Use a waterproof outer in wet weather.

in layers so that you can adjust your insulation according to the work you're doing. A thin waterproof jacket is ideal as an outer skin. I also wouldn't be without a neck gaiter (sometimes called a 'headover'), which keeps your neck

warm and can be pulled up over your head if temperatures really drop. A warm hat is the final essential – but be prepared to strip off this and many other items listed here when you pick up your fork and begin to dig!

▼ The walk to my allotment is usually the coldest part of the visit.

▼ You'll be surprised how quickly the layers come off as the physical work begins!

Grow herbs on your windowsill

N O SELF–RESPECTING cook would be without a good supply of fresh herbs, but there are very few that grow naturally over winter. Supermarkets overcome this problem by buying plants grown under glass, but you can easily extend the growing season yourself in much the same way.

The seeds of annual herbs (that is herbs that germinate, grow, set seed and die all in a single year) are programmed to come to life in spring as the weather warms up. This is why they are much cheaper to buy in summer – pretty much anyone can grow them this way. By sowing them now and fooling them that spring is in the air, you can guarantee a supply for your kitchen all through the colder months. To do this, sow a couple of good pinches of seed (quite thickly in other words) in each of several small pots, cover with less than 10mm (½in) of compost, water (but not too much) and cover the pots with food wrap. This traps the moisture so your seeds won't dry out. The covered pots should be stored somewhere warm – with a consistent temperature of 18–20°C (64–68°F) – but not necessarily light, so an airing cupboard would be ideal.

Germination times vary from one or two days for chives right up to six weeks for parsley. Check the pots every day and immediately move any that show signs of growth to a bright windowsill.

▼ **Herbs take up very little room and are easy to grow, yet they offer the cook so much.**

▲ **Coriander is a wonderful herb. Make successional sowings if you use it regularly.**

Light is all-important now, with four hours of sunlight being a daily minimum and six being preferable. Temperature fluctuations should also be avoided, so watch out for chilly drafts or hot radiators.

As the seedlings mature, pluck out the weaker ones to give their stronger siblings more room to grow. These thinnings can be eaten as can leaves from the remaining plants as they get bigger. It is more productive to pick a leaf or two from each stem than to pull up a whole plant in one go; gentle harvesting encourages fresh new growth.

Five to try

Chives Great in salads, soups and sandwiches, chives need quite warm conditions to keep going in winter. Harvest the young leaves a few at a time by snipping off with scissors.

Coriander Also known as cilantro, this pungent plant is invaluable in Indian, Thai and Mexican cookery. The leaves will not regrow once cut, so it's a good idea to sow a few pots and use up each one in a single harvest.

Mint A vigorous and adaptable herb that can be grown from seed or from 100mm (4in) pieces of root cut from an existing plant. Just cover the roots with a few handfuls of soil, and you'll have baby leaves in six to eight weeks.

Parsley Not the easiest to grow, but certainly worthwhile. To improve your success rate, soak the seeds overnight in warm water and give them plenty of heat once sown. A heated propagator tray is a good idea.

Thyme Buy young plants of this and other perennial herbs (including rosemary, bay and sage) rather than growing from seed. They will be very happy on a windowsill, offering a few leaves as and when you need them, and they can be planted outdoors in spring.

▼ **Mint and chives make great garnishes, and there's no substitute for those flavours.**

▼ **A fresh crop of parsley is well worth the effort that it takes to grow.**

Building terraced raised beds

THE IDEA of raised beds is straightforward: four planks screwed together to lift the ground nearer to the gardener and to allow him or her a degree of control over the growing conditions. They even look nice, so why would you do anything else? Of course, things are never that simple, but that doesn't mean they're not worth pursuing. On my plot (and, I've no doubt, on many others) the ground is quite steeply sloped, which makes any kind of construction rather more complicated. Furthermore, the slope faces the cold north–east, and this has a major effect on the amount of light falling on my crops. The solution here is to terrace the beds, cutting each one into the slope so that the surface of the growing medium remains flat and the beds gradually step down the hill.

▼ **These beds step gently down to compensate for the gradual slope.**

1 DIG A trench along the high side of the bed, so that the bottom of the trench is level with the ground on the lower side.

2 PLACE THE timber for one long wall of the bed into the trench and check it is level and stable. This timber must be pressure treated.

3 FOR THE ends of the bed, dig a trench that is deeper at the high end and level with the ground at the low end. Check the level as before.

4 WHEN ALL four sides of the bed are in place, screw them together and check levels, padding underneath the wood with soil as required.

5 BACKFILL ANY unsightly gaps around the outside of the bed with earth, treading the soil down firmly to ensure it doesn't settle unevenly.

6 FORK OVER the base of the bed and then fill it up with your preferred mix of topsoil, compost, sand and manure, mixing together well.

Insulating plants

▲ Small trees and shrubs can be protected in-situ from wind, rain and cold damage.

▲ If you don't have room for potted plants indoors, they can still be saved from the cold with a little insulation.

WHILE ALLOTMENT gardening is traditionally all about growing staple foods such as onions, brassicas and potatoes, there can be few among us who have never been tempted by the charms of more exotic produce. Our warming British climate now allows us to try lemons and limes, apricots, soya beans, okra and more, but the perennial subjects will most likely require

▼ You can buy insulating materials in garden centres, Make sure they're tied firmly (not too tightly) in place.

some form of protection over winter. There are three aspects of inclement weather that you need to watch out for: wind, rain and cold. The wind can strip leaves, break branches and rock roots in the ground, and it is best tackled with stout stakes and supports. Rain can flood the soil and drown plants – particularly those from drier climates than that of the UK – which may need to be grown in containers and moved under cover. The cold can kill buds and stems by freezing and bursting them apart, and the best way to prevent this is to insulate your tender perennials with a cosy blanket.

You will often see sacking or bubble wrap used for this purpose, but these are less than ideal. Sacking soaks up water and becomes very heavy, while impermeable bubble wrap acts like a sail and can actually increase the chances of wind damage. The best solution is to use a layer or two of horticultural fleece or one of the tailored fleece 'jackets' that slip over the plant and tighten with a drawstring. You can add to the insulating properties of either option by stuffing straw loosely into the interior, creating an extra-warm layer around the branches. A more natural alternative to fleece, which has just recently come on to the market, is jute.

Prepare for the freeze

WE'VE HAD a few mild winters in the UK lately, but there's no telling what we should expect from one year to the next. Apart from your tender plants, there are other parts of the veg garden or allotment to consider. A quick tidy-up of tools and equipment is a good start, and if you're not going to be using them on your plot it might be worth bringing your better tools home, where they can be kept more safely. Raised beds can be prone to weathering at this time of year, with heavy rainfall washing the goodness out of them and winds stripping the top layers. Cover them up with cardboard or plastic sheeting, weighed down well with bricks, recycled plastic bottles filled with water or compost bags filled with earth. Lastly, freezing water is a potential source of damage to your water–collection and irrigation systems, so spend a little time on putting these to bed before any harm is done.

1 MODERN OUTDOOR taps tend to be frost proof, but there are still many in use that could be ruined if the water inside them were to freeze. To avoid this inconvenience, tie an insulating layer of bubble wrap or sacking all around the tap. It must be good and thick – so that you can't tell there's a tap underneath.

2 WRAP UP any pipes running along outside walls, both to your tap and away from it if the supply goes on somewhere else. This is an easy job thanks to the invention of polythene pipe lagging – essentially a tube of insulation that keeps the pipes snug. Pipes coming up from the ground can be treated this way, too.

3 IN A really cold winter your water butt may freeze over, and the ice has the potential to force open plumbing joints, damage taps and even split the sides of a plastic tub. As you won't need much water through the winter, the simplest solution is just to leave the tap open and allow the butt to drain.

4 DON'T FORGET to empty garden hoses for the same reasons. Do this by opening the nozzle at the end and laying the whole length out as flat as possible to let trapped pockets of water escape. Putting the reel up high (on a table perhaps) before slowly winding the hose back in gives any last traces a helping hand.

Increasing water storage

▲ Water butt connection kits like this one cost very little and are easy to install.

▲ Butts should be level or step down slightly to make the most of storage space.

COLLECTING RAINWATER is very sensible even if you have a standpipe or water trough close to your plot. Not only is it better for the environment than using heavily treated tap water, it is also generally better for your plants, particularly ericaceous shrubs like blueberries. The main problem for many gardeners is storing it; a single 210l (44gal/55gal US) water butt fed from a shed roof can fill up in minutes, but if the weather turns hot and dry this reserve will only last a week or so on an allotment.

A canny solution is to add extra water butts, each fed from the overflow of the last so that you catch much more water during periods of rainfall. As you'll have emptied your existing butts (see previous project), now is the time to extend your storage. The butts should be situated next to one another, ideally all at the same level or slowly stepping down from one butt to the next. If any butt is higher than the previous one, it won't fill up to its maximum capacity. Join them together with a simple, inexpensive linking kit.

Another idea is to buy a bigger water butt, and these are now available with huge capacities upwards of 1,000l (210gal/260gal US). Such big tanks can be expensive but will save you the hassle of extra plumbing and look rather neater and more professional than a line of smaller butts. Be aware that a large volume of water can be very heavy – the 1,000l (210gal/260gal US) butt will weigh around a tonne, so will need to be placed on solid ground. For irrigating my salad beds at home, I splashed out (sorry) on a wooden-panelled design that blends nicely with the rest of the garden.

▼ Large capacity tanks don't need to look ugly, and are worth the extra expense if you have a large plot.

Jobs for mid-winter

Feeling Fruity

The space available on most allotments allows you to be adventurous when it comes to choosing what you grow. Why not consider asking your family to chip in for a fruit cage this Christmas?

Batten Down the Hatches

A summer of enthusiastic use can take its toll on sheds and greenhouses. To keep out the damaging winter weather, make time to repair any loose roofing felt and replace broken glass panels. By the time the weather improves you'll be too busy planting to get these jobs done.

Bird Brained

If you think there's little to be had from a winter allotment, spare a thought for the birds. They will greatly appreciate anything you leave out for them, and will reward you in spring by decimating slug, aphid and mosquito populations. Don't forget that water can also be hard to come by on a frozen morning.

A Tool Inspection

Now that your tools have been laid aside for winter, it's a good time to inspect them for faults and make repairs. If the prospect of dismantling, oiling and cleaning your power tools is too daunting, consider having them professionally serviced. This will cost around £50 and should include blade sharpening and balancing, a filter clean, oil change and general health check. For smaller power tools, expect to pay a bit less for routine maintenance and repairs. Giving your garden equipment an annual check is likely to save you money in the long term and means you can make a flying start on your spring jobs!

Drink Problem

Take the time to walk around your plot on a damp evening, squashing any slugs and snails you find. Of course, you won't get them all, so set beer traps in each bed and prime them with a dose of cheap lager or even leftover slops from drip trays in pubs – if you're not too embarrassed to ask for them!

Late Winter

Even the most dedicated gardeners need a bit of encouragement to get them outside at this time of year; not only is it still cold and windy but the weather has a tendency to turn wet as well. It's not all bad news, though, as the first signs of spring are all around if you know where to look. While it may be a subtle change, that just makes it all the more exciting when you see it. Early flowers and bulbs make a welcome appearance, and the branches of every tree seem ready to burst into life. The trick to getting some useful gardening done now is to wait until you have a few days of good weather. If your soil isn't too wet you can still fit in that last bit of digging, and beds prepared now will be ready for planting come the spring.

▼ As your plants don't need any attention at this time of year, it's good to get the rest of the plot into shape.

▲ These fantastic dahlias will grace any village show, and are not difficult to look after.

Plant summer-flowering bulbs

ONE TRADITIONAL part of the allotment that modern plot–holders often neglect is the cutting garden. If your patch isn't limited to being a ready source of fresh and tasty food, it can also supply beautiful cut flowers to brighten your home. This makes for great conversations at dinner parties (not only did you grow the meal, but the table display too!), and can save you a packet compared with the prices at the florist's.

As with growing fruit and veg, you need to plan in advance. The flowers beginning to show their heads at this time of year were probably planted in the autumn, but you can get started now on designing a summer display. While planting in earnest won't start until early spring (March in the UK), get ahead by forcing some bulbs indoors. Dahlia tubers and gladioli corms can be covered with a thin layer of multipurpose compost in a shallow tray, then left somewhere light and warm (around 10°C/50°F) to encourage them to sprout before planting outside. Stop them drying out by misting with a spray gun. For a mobile display, plant up containers with lily and Dutch iris bulbs now, then take the whole pot home when they're ready to flower in the summer – perfect for brightening a patio.

▲ Plant a variety of bulbs for an extended display. Gladioli are classic late-summer flowers.

▼ Irises are available in a huge range of colours and sizes, with flowering times from early spring to summer.

Spring-flowering bulbs

Some spring-flowering bulbs such as snowdrops are sold 'in the green', which means they have already flowered and still have some foliage. They should be planted quickly, at the same depth as they were previously growing. Buy from a reputable supplier to ensure the bulbs haven't been harvested illegally from the wild.

sprouting seeds

EVEN IN the depths of winter it is perfectly possible to grow fresh food from seed. While the garden might be a little inhospitable, the kitchen windowsill is warm and bright enough for plants to germinate. By choosing the right kind of seeds you can enjoy fresh salad greens year round – just don't wait for them to grow to full size!

If what you want to do is spice up your sandwiches, cress is a great way to start. All you need is a saucer lined with kitchen towel, cotton wool or even an old flannel. Moisten your chosen medium and simply sprinkle with the cress seeds. Cover with a plastic bag then place in a warm spot such as the airing cupboard until the seeds have germinated. When the seedlings begin to emerge, place on a well–lit windowsill

▲ **A quick rinse under the tap, once or twice a day, is all the maintenance sprouting seeds require.**

▼ **A sprouting kit with several trays allows you to keep an ongoing supply of fresh greens.**

▲ **As the sprouts develop, their flavour will change. Eat yours whenever you think they're at their best.**

and remove the plastic covering. Ensure that the medium is kept moist, and you'll be enjoying the fresh sprouts in 10 to 14 days.

If you want to get a little more involved, a seed sprouter is the way forward. Typically consisting of three or four perforated trays over a drip catcher, these simple devices take up very little room in the kitchen. A rinse under the tap each morning and evening is all that's necessary to bring the seeds to life, and the multiple trays allow you to grow a succession of seeds (either all the same or mixed) so that you have a constant supply of mature sprouts.

▼ **Nutritious and flavoursome, sprouted seeds transform a green salad and can be harvested year round.**

Try these...

Alfalfa Perhaps the quintessential sprouting seed, packed with nutrients and with a sweet flavour, it is extra-quick growing, and alfalfa seeds are ready to eat in between two and four days.

Beet The young red shoots are certainly pretty enough to garnish any plate, and the flavour (which is just like fresh beetroot) is a delicious addition to any salad dish.

Brassica 'Hot Stuff' Most brassicas make for good sprouting, but this named variety has a unique spicy flavour. Delicious in sandwiches, this is best grown in the same way as standard cress.

Mung Beans The ever-popular Chinese beansprouts are very high in vitamin C, among other good things. Great eaten raw, they are also a good addition to stir fries and soups.

Radish You don't need to let these grow large before they develop their distinctive flavour. Two to six days is all the shoots require.

Snow Peas These have a sweeter taste than green peas but take slightly longer than most to reach the edible stage. They are well worth the 7–10 days' wait, though!

Making paths

▲ **Good access to all parts of your plot will save you lots of time; it's worth getting this right early on.**

THE BEST way to set off well-groomed raised beds is with a neat and durable path. This makes access simple and reduces weeding. Paths can be made from old timber, paving slabs or anything else you have lying around, but I like to do a proper, permanent job to save trouble later on. A path built on a firm, well-drained base with no weeds is one of those things you rarely notice but which makes every other job much easier.

Good paths can consist of gravel, wood chip, brick or one of countless other landscaping materials, but all share some basic characteristics.

They should be wide enough for a wheelbarrow (remember you'll need to turn around somewhere) and should give unrestricted access to every inch of your veg plot. You'll want paths to be low maintenance, so they should exclude weeds. Drainage is also an issue – will water collect in low spots after heavy rainfall? Nobody wants to wade through a bog to pick their beans. Remember some materials, particularly timber, can be slippery when wet.

1 LEVEL THE ground and remove any large stones. If you have heavy soil, mixing in some sharp sand will help drainage. Dig up any perennial weeds; these are most likely to break through the path. Firm the soil well. This path is designed to be used with raised beds; if you don't have these in place, build them first.

2 WEED-EXCLUDING FABRIC is available in a variety of sizes. Lay it along the paths, taking care not to leave holes where light might shine through. Be aware that heavy work boots can easily tear this material, and the wind can snatch it, so be sure to weigh it down as necessary.

3 THE EDGES of a path are often the point where weeds appear. You'll save time in the long run if you carefully push the edges of the weed-excluding fabric underneath the timber of the raised beds, again being careful not to tear it with your fingers or shoes.

4 NOW THE satisfying part. Fill the paths with your choice of mulch, to a depth of at least 50mm (2in) – more for lighter materials. This thickness will kill weeds by blocking out light and will also protect the fabric from wear. Rake level and tamp down firmly.

Crop rotation

IT USED to be commonplace to grow crops in the same spot from one year to the next, allowing you to tailor the soil conditions to a permanently resident plant. These days, however, we realize that pests and disease can build up in the soil and the nutrients required for growth will gradually be depleted. Rather than dig new veg beds every year, a simple system of crop rotation requires nothing more than a little forward planning.

The technique is called rotation because each type of crop is moved from one part of the veg patch to the next in successive seasons. Some people use a three-year rotation, some wait as long as six, but four is a happy medium and fits well with the main plant families.

All you need to do is divide your growing space into four and then keep each family (described below) restricted to one quarter. With each new growing season you circulate the crops, so that each quarter of the plot hosts the next family on the list. The order of rotation is a subject of great dispute, but the most important thing is to choose a sequence and stick to it.

▼ **Keeping each plant family together and moving them from year to year is good for plants and soil.**

Top three reasons for rotating your crops

Soil structure Depending on what you started with, it can take many years to get a really good soil in place. While an initial dig is usually the best way to start new beds, by growing different crops in successive seasons you can create a good balance with the minimum effort. Potatoes have dense foliage that shades out weeds, and they require plenty of digging, which opens up the ground. Brassicas, meanwhile, will enjoy plenty of compost, which is a sure-fire way to improve soil structure and chemistry.

Nutrition Different families of plants make varying demands on the soil – from the basic requirements of plant growth (nitrogen, phosphorous and potassium) to trace minerals such as iron and zinc. If the same plants are grown repeatedly in the same patch of ground, it stands to reason that the nutrients they require will be depleted. By circulating your crops you allow natural processes to replace what has been used up.

Plant health The number-one advantage of moving crops around your plot is that you'll give pests and diseases very little chance of building up to problem levels. Soil-dwelling nasties like clubroot, eelworm and white rot will be much less likely to appear if their target species is only present one season in four.

Legumes – An important family in the crop–rotation cycle, legumes include all sorts of podded veg from broad, runner and French beans to peas and green manures like clover and alfalfa.

Onion family – Bulb and salad onions are included here, also shallots and garlic. Don't forget leeks, which are obviously related when you consider their habit.

Carrot and **Tomato** families – Carrots, parsnips, celery, peppers, tomatoes and potatoes make up this diverse but very useful group. Many of these are particularly prone to soil–borne pests.

Brassicas – Cabbages, cauliflowers and Brussels sprouts are obviously close relatives, but also covered here are swedes, turnips and radishes.

▼ **Beans and peas actively improve the ground in which they grow, fixing nitrogen from the air into the soil.**

Prepare beds for early sowing

AT THIS time of year, plot-holders will often compete to be the first to get crops in the ground. While sowing too early can be counter-productive, with any late frost putting paid to your hard work, there are advantages to an early start. You will be extending the growing season, allowing you to squeeze more productivity out of the space available to you, but perhaps less obvious is the boost this gives your plants in the battle against pests and disease. If you can get your seedlings going early, they will with luck be well advanced when trouble arrives. Pests are much more likely to go for younger, more tender plants than those that are reaching maturity.

One of the best ways to increase early growth rates is to warm up the soil in your beds. Simply covering your beds with an insulating layer of plastic encourages germination and can fool the young plants into thinking conditions are better than they really are.

1 IF YOU haven't already dug your beds, clear away any debris or weeds remaining from last season and give the ground a good forking over to break up larger clods. Rake the soil roughly level.

2 CUT A sheet of clear polythene to size (available from garden centres and DIY stores) and lay over your growing area. The thicker the material, the more insulating (and long lasting) it will be.

3 HOLD THE polythene in place with bricks, or by 'stapling' it into the soil using tent pegs or bits of wire coat hanger cut and bent into shape. Be thorough here, or the wind will whip the plastic away.

4 AFTER A few weeks, when you are ready to sow or plant out, remove the cover and hoe the ground well. Any weeds that have germinated in the warmth will then be killed off before they grow.

Jobs for late winter

Dig This
If you haven't quite got around to digging over that last bed, it's not too late. Granted, you've missed the hardest frosts, which would have helped break the soil down and kill pests, but if the ground isn't too wet it's still well worthwhile.

Pipe Dream
If you have any kind of water-collection system set up, it's a good idea to check it's working well and not leaking anywhere. Spring showers won't last for ever, and by the time summer arrives you'll be grateful for any rainwater you can catch.

Beat the Queues
If you want to avoid disappointment, it's worth getting on the phone and ordering your seed potatoes right away. Demand is about to rocket, and growers tend to have limited stocks of anything new or unusual – which, of course, tend to be the most sought-after varieties.

Fenced In
As the weather gets warmer, the chances of vandals taking an interest in your plot will increase. Most allotments are protected by fences and gates, but these are often in a poor state. Take the time to contact the landowner and ask them to repair any breaks, or, if it comes to it, make the rounds yourself and patch up the defences.

Stock Up
If you're organized you will have ordered your seed supplies last year. There are other things to consider now, though: do you have enough seed compost, planting trays and modules, root trainers and so on?

Give Me Shelter
One of the biggest killers of early crops are cold winds, which can sweep across an open allotment site at speed. Protect your seedlings by creating a windbreak of old pallets or specialized wind fencing.

Recommended suppliers

THESE ARE the companies I tend to use for all my seeds, plants, tools and gardening sundries (in no particular order). There are, of course, many others, some of which are also very good.

The Organic Gardening Catalogue

This is, pretty much, what you might expect! Everything you could possibly need to run an organic garden or allotment, at fair prices and from a reliable supplier. Seeds, books, tools and more.
+44 (0)845 130 1304
www.organiccatalogue.com

Thompson & Morgan

A long-established and respected company with one of the best ranges of seeds and young plants. They have many exclusive varieties, not to mention a reputation for quality.
+ 44 (0)1473 695 225
www.thompson-morgan.com
www.tmseeds.com
www.tandmworldwide.com

Marshalls

Another reputable seed supplier, currently taking great interest in the 'grow-your-own' market. The Marshalls catalogue is practically fought over in our house – it's beautifully illustrated and very easy to use.
+44 (0)1480 443 390
www.marshalls-seeds.co.uk

Harrod Horticultural

A tempting crop of top-end equipment, from raised beds and fruit cages to tools, gloves and boots. Not the cheapest, but good value in the long run. Will give your plot a professional touch.
+44 (0)845 402 5300
www.harrodhorticultural.com

Haxnicks

A useful company offering an authoritative range of garden fabrics (such as fleece, insect mesh, polythene sheeting and weed-proof membrane) as well as cloches, plant tunnels and more.
+44 (0)845 241 1555
www.haxnicks.co.uk

Makita

My first choice for power tools of the DIY sort (as opposed to garden machinery). Simple, intelligent designs and reliable engineering. They have a new range of cordless tools with smaller, lighter but more powerful batteries. How I love them.
+44 (0)1908 211 678
www.makitauk.com
www.makita.com

Stihl

Designed for the professional, but within the budget of most keen gardeners, Stihl tools have never failed to impress me. My favourite has to be their combi-system – a neat and powerful engine with a variety of useful attachments – strimmer, cultivator, hedge trimmer, etc.
+44 (0)1276 202 02
www.stihl.co.uk
www.stihl.com

Helpful Organizations

The Green Shopping Catalogue

In my view, this is the best collection of books on subjects such as organic gardening, crafting, sustainable living and so on. Also a brilliant range of unusual tools, garden and household items with an ecological flavour.
+44 (0)1730 823 311
www.green-shopping.co.uk

Kore Wild Fruit Nursery

A small, mail-order nursery that specializes in unusual edible plants from all over the world. Whether you're after a thimbleberry, a prickly pear or a raisin tree, look no further!
+44 (0)1600 860 248
www.korewildfruitnursery.co.uk

Agroforestry Research Trust

A great resource for those who have little time to maintain their edible garden. Agroforestry is all about creating natural, woodland-style landscapes using edible and medicinal plants.
+44 (0)1803 840 776
www.agroforestry.co.uk

The Real Seed Company

A private collection of rare, heirloom and unusual vegetables now made available to the public. Perfect for anyone who values flavour and nutrition above perfectly-shaped, supermarket-style food.
+44 (0)1239 821 107
www.realseeds.co.uk

National Society of Allotment and Leisure Gardeners (NSALG)

+ 44 (0)1536 266 576
www.nsalg.org.uk/

Garden Organic

+44 (0)24 7630 3517
www.gardenorganic.org.uk

Royal Horticultural Society (RHS)

+44 (0)845 062 1111
www.rhs.org.uk

Allotments Regeneration Initiative (ARI)

www.farmgarden.org.uk/ari

Scottish Allotments and Gardens Society (SAGS)

www.sags.org.uk

National Allotment Gardens Trust

www.nagtrust.org

About the author

PAUL WAGLAND is an RHS-qualified gardener and an experienced writer and designer. He specializes in the practical side of horticulture, from growing fruit and vegetables to landscaping and outdoor DIY. With a firm belief that allotment gardening can provide answers to many of today's problems (obesity and other health issues, food miles and pollution, work–life balance and much more) Paul has redesigned and renovated various neglected plots for pleasure, and even profit. He is the former editor of two popular gardening magazines (*Pond & Gardening* and *Grow Your Own*) and divides most of his free time between his own garden and three allotments in suburban Essex.

Index

To place an order, or to request a catalogue, contact:
GMC Publications
Castle Place, 166 High Street, Lewes, East Sussex, BN7 1XU
United Kingdom
Tel: 01273 488005 Fax: 01273 402866
Website: www.gmcbooks.com
Orders by credit card are accepted